ALWAYS LOOKING FORWARD

walter bond

the alf lone wolf

This book is dedicated to the women and men of the Animal Liberation Front.

Sheepskin Factory in Denver

"The arson at the Sheepskin Factory in Denver was done in defense and retaliation for all the innocent animals that have died cruelly at the hands of human oppressors. Be warned that making a living from the use and abuse of animals will not be tolerated. Also be warned that leather is every bit as evil as fur. As demonstrated in my recent arson against the Leather Factory in Salt Lake City. Go Vegan!
- ALF Lone Wolf"

"The Animal Liberation Front is watching and there is nowhere to hide. The arson at the Tiburon restaurant in Sandy Utah was done because of their sale of Foie Gras and other 'wild game.' Animals exist for their own purposes, not human ends. Go Vegan!
- ALF Lone Wolf."

Table of Contents

~ Extras ~

"A Mother's Reflection"

My name is Mickie. Walter Bond is my son. He is a Prisoner Of War for his defense of the Animal Nations. He has been reviled by the press and by those who do not wish to have their consciences tampered with, thereby allowing them to continue to accept the blindness society needs in order for the machine to continue to grind along.

Walter Bond was born a warrior; he did not choose it because he found a worthy or righteous cause. A warrior is born with a fire inside and a need to right wrongs. He is born with a compassion and caring rooted so deeply that it is difficult to walk away from any sort of cruelty, whether it involves the people, the Animal Nations, the oceans and seas or the whole of Mother Earth and Father Sky.

Webster's Dictionary's definition of "warrior" is as follows: 1) a person engaged or experienced in warfare; soldier 2) a person who shows or has shown great vigor, courage or aggressiveness.

Yes, Walter Bond is a warrior. As his mother, I am very proud. As his mother, I want to rant and rave at the world at large. I want to tell them that America is not this politically correct, sensitive, caring place filled with heroes. Why does heroism only apply to humans? Why is little Johnny a hero for helping the elderly lady next door carry her groceries, or help her cross the busy street, or shovel her walkway after a snowfall -- but Walter Bond risks his life and his future to spare animals from imprisonment, torture, horrific daily abuses and is labeled a terrorist, a threat to the well-being of America?

We hear phrases about "the Greening of America," which of course is a fallacy. You hear of all the different appliances that save energy and are kind to the environment. You hear about new sources of energy that are environmentally "friendly," safer building materials, environmentally friendly automobiles, etc. – until your head feels like it wants to explode. The bottom line is that you will then leave a smaller "carbon footprint." What an inane statement that is.

First and foremost, these statements – or rather elitist philosophies – are geared (of course) toward the power mongers. They are the only ones who can afford the twenty, thirty or forty thousand dollars it would take to remodel their homes and turn them into green palaces. An environmentally-friendly home to help save Mother Earth... the Greening of America... what a load of crap. But please let me be politically correct, "what a load of Green Crap."

The machines grind on, the slaughterhouses keep up their daily executions, the so-called research labs continue their torture on the most innocent beings on the earth. After all, without animal testing the cosmetics companies wouldn't be able to insure that the bottle of makeup you just purchased really will hide your blemishes or wrinkles or uneven skin tone, etc., ad nauseum.

Next up is "the dumbing-down of America." Here is my favorite example: politicians. At this point, how can people have faith in any of them? They appear standing on bales of hay, wearing their brad new checkered cotton shirts, brand new jeans and straw summer cowboy hats, and tell you they are just like you... just a hard-working American with simple roots ... memories of fishing down by the "ol' fishing hole" dancing in their heads.

Amazingly, people still believe in them. Folks, look down a little further and you will see that at the bottom of those Levi pant legs, he's wearing $1,000 leather shoes. The only place he's having memories of growing up living that hard-scrabble, yet fulfilling simple life is on his private jet, limo or his third, fourth or fifth summer home, while he is enjoying an afternoon cup of tea.

Here is my own personal observation about the submissiveness of the world: People seem to have given away their power, their uniqueness, their confidence in their beliefs and blindly follow the media, politicians and the mainstream consensus.

I consider what passes for civilization these days to be laughable. I suppose that people as a whole can say, "we live in a civilized state," but do we?... really?

In the Webster's Dictionary, I found two meanings for the word civilized: 1) having an advanced or humane culture, society, etc. 2) easy to manage or control. Here I will put in writing two examples for these definitions, as I understand them...

1) I live in the Alaskan Wilderness with my man, who is my imperfect best friend. We live with our two wolves, which honor us with their presence every day. We live in a one-room cabin with a loft. We haul water, use an outhouse. Like all animals in the wild, we are part of the food chain. Like all animals who live in harmony with our Mother Earth, we respect each other's territories. We mind to our own ways and sometimes we fight each other to survive or sometimes we simply let the other know "this is my territory... you must leave." We all endure our struggles with the winter snows, the cold, the summer floods, the river's rage. Some of us live through these times, some of us do not. These are the cycles of Mother Earth for the two-leggeds, the four-leggeds and our flying relatives. We risk, we struggle, we enjoy the bounties of our Mother. We survive from year to year, or not. These are the natural rhythms of life. I chose this life because it is a truly civilized society – balanced, humane, respectful of the Mother of us all. All animals have the right to be free, to live and die on their own terms, because of their ability to survive, not caged from birth to feed the lazy and the gluttonous.

There is that other definition of civilized: 2) easy to manage and control.

Watch out folks, the edible ones first... who's second? Do people packed into apartments in overcrowded cities with just enough money or means to get by, but not enough to move themselves or their children into happy, healthy natural environments ring a bell?... Easy to control?

- - - - - - - - - - - - - - - -

How do I feel about my son being imprisoned for standing up for those without a voice, without power to fight back, those whose suffering doesn't end until death grants them mercy?

I feel at peace and successful as a parent, because when it is time for me to make the spirit journey, I will know the Animal Nations have a truly civilized human being among them – Walter Bond.

And so it is…
Mickie Coyote

- *Introduction* -

In the summer of 2010, I was arrested in Denver, Colorado for setting fire to three businesses across two states: The Sheepskin Factory in Denver, The Leather Factory in Salt Lake City, Utah and Tiburon Restaurant in Sandy, Utah, which sold foie gras and other once vibrant wild and exotic animals.

This, however, was not my first brush with the law. In the winter of 1997, I was arrested for burning down the home and methamphetamine operation of a millionaire drug dealer. What came to be known as an act of Straight Edge justice was really just a desperate attempt to save my brother from a life of addiction. Ironically, that same brother would be the informant in my string of Animal Liberation Front arsons, after he learned there was a reward for my arrest.

On July 22 of 2010, I began my county jail time. I spent nearly a year and a half in jail before ever stepping foot back into prison. Much of that time was spent in boring lockdown units around petty criminals and detoxing heroin addicts. Always hating to be idle, I began writing public statements, essays and articles… all of which turned into the book in your hands. I figured it was my duty to do so. So few Prisoners Of War and political prisoners speak out for themselves, especially Animal Liberation Front activists.

Many moons ago, when I was a wee little Vegan, I remember reading the essays of the A.L.F. warrior Rod Coronado. I remember the profound impact those writings had on me. Not because of their eloquence, but because of the spirit of resistance that inspired them. I felt as though Rod was speaking directly to me and challenging me to commit myself with actions instead of mere words. As of the time of this writing, I recently re-read Rod's book, "Flaming Arrows," and it speaks more to me now than it ever did before. Once again, I felt the voice of understanding, but this time it was with my plight as an imprisoned warrior.

It is for both of these reasons that this book of my

collected essays has been put to print: so that you current and future Vegan warriors need never feel alone. So that you may know that though we may never see total victory in our lifetimes, victory is ours just by fighting. By breaking the chains that bind us in submissiveness. Reclaiming our ferocity and literally freeing the Animals and turning on their exploiters. I also purposefully wrote articles of a personal nature, explaining who I am and some of my worldviews, not because I personally feel like I'm that interesting of a person, but to show you that I am a person. To put more of a three dimensional aspect to one person behind the mask, in hopes that you can identify with me instead of placing me on the mantle of hero.

I am nothing if not approachable, curious and flawed. Also, in my writings you will find a worldview with more than one influence. I have been a punk rock teenager, an angry straight edge kid and a Vegan Hardliner. I have worked building slaughterhouses and worked in health food stores. I have been influenced deeply by biocentrism, anti-civilization, eco-anarchism, and various politically charged bands from Bob Marley to Vegan Reich. Not to mention years of Vegan outreach and work at various Animal sanctuaries.

If there is one thing I pride myself on and you, oh Reader, can take comfort in, it's that the words you will read in this slim volume come from someone that is a grassroots street-level activist. All too often, in the human movement for Animal Liberation, we exalt the poet over the warrior, the website over the manual, the scholar over the experienced, and our abstractions over our feelings of right and wrong. I have often been asked if I think my way is the only way. Of course, I don't. I have also been asked if I think everyone should join the Animal Liberation Front. Of course, I do!

The great truths of life are revealed in brevity. And one of those truths is that "Animals deserve to live free of human use and abuse." Another truth is "you get out of things what you put into them." If activism doesn't feel like hard work and sacrifice, then it's not the true selfless work of

Animal Liberation. Don't ask me how you can help Animals, I showed you better that I could tell you. Instead ask yourself, "What the fuck am I waiting for?"

Animal Liberation, Whatever It May Take!

Regards,
Walter Bond
ALF-POW

WALTER BOND
ALF-POW
X LONE V WOLF X

For Grahm (Walter's Background Story)

On the Second of September, 2010, my grandmother, Gwen Bond, passed away in Mason City, IA. I regret not being by her side when she went, but I regret even more that I could not be there to console my father, James L. Bond (yes, my father's name is actually James Bond). He was always very close with his mother and I know it is a hard time for him, as having not only lost his mom but also having his son imprisoned at the same time together create quite a tribulation for him.

Gwen, or Grahm as we all called her, was the last of my grandparents to pass. She will be missed by many in north Iowa, as she was the life of the party – literally singing and dancing the night away well into her 80s. She was also a friend to any cat who crossed her path. My grandmother had two homes, one in Mason City and one in Clear Lake, IA, which was a cottage. At the cottage she diligently cared for 8 indoor cats, fed the strays in the neighborhood, and provided food for the ferals in the woods around her property.

Her home in Mason City was damaged by flooding a few years back. This forced her to move in with my father at his adjoining property. She never allowed the house to be destroyed though. Since she could not live there, she donated it to the cats. She would have my father walk her over several times a week to visit them. My grandmother taught me that the very best way to fall asleep is with a cat on your chest, one on your legs, and perhaps another one by your side. Wherever you are, Grahm, I will miss you and I know the cats do too.

I want to say thank you to everyone who has written me and continues to write. Words cannot describe how much your correspondence and support mean to me. A big thank you to all my comrades across the pond in the UK who have written and sent me Vegan support zines, which I have received. Although I may be by myself, I am not alone!

My "Why I'm Vegan" essay is beginning to grab the attention of many in the mainstream press, including Fox

News, which recently approached me for an interview. I now have a support site (SupportWalter.org) to which I submit an occasional rant.

I'm scheduled for court on November 11th, 2010 for a change of plea hearing. This court date should be set, but if it changes I will get the word out ASAP. Whether I spend time in prison or not, any legal defense money raised for me will either be used for a paid attorney or to fight my appeals. I'm requesting that 10% of any money raised for my legal defense go to support imprisoned Earth and Animal Liberation Warriors in Mexico.

As always, the fight goes on. Animals used for food, entertainment, vivisection, and clothing are abused and exploited in the worst imaginable ways. Their suffering is no mere abstraction or matter of philosophy. It is not rhetorical or subjective. It is actual and evil!

For the countless billions who have died, have a sense of urgency. For the scores of billions who will die this year, whom we can't save, have a sense of urgency! There is no excuse for apathy, Vegan or otherwise. Potlucks and picnics do not stop the shackle, the chain fall, the battery cage or the LD-50. People who profit off the blood trade won't stop because the righteousness of our cause overcomes their hard-heartedness.

Let me make it clear that until every cage is empty, we will fight and educate.

Animal Liberation, whatever it may take!

It Is Not a Metaphorical Holocaust
that They Suffer...

My name is Walter Bond and I am currently incarcerated in Golden, Colorado for alleged A.L.F. activity. The mainstream media has done its best to vilify and discredit me. Not at all surprising since we Animal Liberationist activists represent a threat to the status quo and the blood trades they currently support. Therefore any Animal Liberation activist who is effectively standing up against these mechanized evils is going to face government intimidation and persecution.

I am undeterred and unbowed in my desire to live in a world free from Animal abuse and exploitation. And so I would like to say a few brief words to my supporters and to my enemies.

I am Vegan and Straight Edge. I have been for 15 years and will remain so until the day I die. Although I hope to not spend several years of my life in prison, nothing that the United States government does to me will ever equal or even compare to the everyday holocaust that Animals suffer in the name of food, clothing, product testing and entertainment. And I assure you, it is not a metaphorical holocaust that they suffer. I have seen it with my own eyes. When I was 19, I worked for a crew that built slaughterhouses in the Midwest. The horrors I witnessed there I will never forget. That is why and how I became an Animal Rights activist.

To my supporters: Do what you can to raise awareness about the plight of farmed Animals, the environmental and ethical impacts of Animal exploitation, and the positive impact of Veganism. To have a greater knowledge of these issues than the general public and not speak out is complicity. Please do not be complicit in the holocaust against Animals and the Earth.

To my detractors: Take a look at what you are defending. If it's not wrong to use and exploit Animals, then go visit a slaughter house and see for yourselves what happens behind those walls. If you can't eat your meal and view how it's produced at the same time, then eating Animals is very clearly wrong.

Just because we as individuals and societies have the ability to exploit Animals does not give us the right to do so.

Once upon a time it was acceptable for men to exploit women and those who stood against it were considered criminals. Now women can vote, read, and work.

Once upon a time it was legal to own human slaves and those who stood against it were beaten, imprisoned, and murdered. Now that level of racism is unthinkable.

Today Animals are the oppressed and the excuses to use them are the same excuses the slave-owners used. Those excuses are equally invalid when applied to Animal enslavement and exploitation.

Why I Am Vegan

In the winter of 1995, when I was 19 years old, I got a job with a company by the name of Dakota Mechanical. We built slaughter-houses in the Midwest, mainly in Iowa. The state of Iowa is the largest producer of pork in the nation. At the time I was employed in that evil industry there were 27 slaughter-houses for pigs alone. I helped build the IBP plant in Logansport, Indiana as well. It was a brand new plant.

I never saw an Animal murdered in the 9 or so months I worked in Logansport, but it wasn't difficult for me to get the gist of what many of those machines would do when in operation. I was primarily a forklift operator to begin with, but then worked my way to industrial plumber's apprentice. After that factory was built there was a three month layoff.
But soon I got the call for the next job. The one that would forever change my life. It was a smaller job; we were to build an extension to the kill floor at the IBP plant in Perry, Iowa. In this fully functioning slaughter-house I saw the most grizzly mechanized murders that there are to witness. Since it was an old facility we were constantly called away from our construction work to do maintenance throughout the plant. From the pen runs, to the kill floor, to rendering, over the course of 5 months I was a confederate and accomplice to it all.

When I first started the smells, sights, and sounds were overbearing. I kept telling myself, "This is what you eat; don't get squeamish." Within 6 to 8 weeks I felt soul dead. For 12 hours a day, sometimes 15, I often worked ankle deep in gore.

Like the 3 days I worked plumbing rinse stations with 40 gallon drums of de-skinned hogs' heads staring at me.
Or the times I would have to take the forklift behind the facility to gather raw materials, right next to which was a 25 foot pile of 'defective' hogs which were 'unfit for human consumption.' For one reason or another they were left in

heaping piles, exposed to the elements and freezing to death in the Iowa cold. With all the horrors to which I was privy, it's that pile of freezing dead that still haunts my soul.

Then came the day that changed me. We were wrapping up all our tools and cleaning up when a hog who had been knocked out with an electric jolt, had his throat stuck, and had been hung upside down to bleed to death woke up, convulsed, and freed himself of the foot-hold. He came running off of the kill floor straight toward me and the rest of the crew. Three IBP workers gave chase. One with a pipe wrench and two with baseball bats. They began to beat the hog to death. I turned away as I thought anyone would... I was wrong. As I turned, I was face to face with the rest of my crew. While listening to the thuds and squeals of a blunt force death a mere 30 feet behind me, I watched as my co-workers whooped and cheered, high-fiving each other each time there was a thud, laughing and celebrating the violent death of a sentient being.

That night in my hotel room my mind raced. I was disgusted with myself. I was disgusted with humanity. I quit eating meat. A few days later my foreman approached me and asked if I need to borrow any money. I said, "No, why do you ask?" He said that he'd noticed that all I'd been eating was peanut butter and jelly and that he thought I was broke. I told him that I wasn't broke and that I was simply done eating meat. He began heckling me and calling me a "born-again tree hugger." I quit on the spot.

I went home and began to study Animal Rights. I went Vegan and became active in a legal capacity. I spent years tabling and talking with people. I worked at Animal sanctuaries and rescued Animals whenever I could.

I have never felt that anything I have done or will do on behalf of our Mother Earth and her Animal Nations has been enough. Those machines I built back in 1996 are still murdering, even as I write this. That is my guilt and my shame; I earned them. But it is also my strength and resolve. Nothing will ever make me forget the plight of factory farmed Animals and so-called free range, which is just as sick, wrong, unnecessary, and indefensible.

Like all industries of Animal exploitation, the circle of abuse will end with the antagonist (humans) falling prey to its own perfidiousness. For instance, my grandfather was a hog farmer whom I never met. He died in the year of my birth, after the ammonia from hog waste destroyed his lungs. That same waste run-off from his and adjoining hog farms in the 70s poisoned the ground water, allowing illegal levels of radium to pollute the tap water. To this day in certain areas of the Midwest you have to sign a waiver stating that the water from public works is hazardous to your health and that you are "OK" with that before they will turn your water on.

I've said it before, but it's worth restating. It is these industries of death that are the Animal and Earth terrorists. Not those who fight against them.

Defiance In the Face of Adversity

In this essay, I'm going to delve into a much-neglected topic in the underground, namely remaining stouthearted after an arrest. It's a touchy subject that I feel qualified to address. So before I get into the bulk of what I have to say, let me throw my own credentials on the table. I'm not trying to impress as much as verify that I have earned the right to critique on this subject.

In the winter of 1997, I was convicted of arson in Mason City, Iowa for burning down the house of convicted drug dealer Steve Gomez and the methamphetamine operation in that house. I was pretty much caught in the act, being as he was under federal investigation for selling large amounts of meth and I was younger and acted purely on emotion, throwing all caution to the wind. This was my introduction to the criminal injustice system.

Then as now, a whole circus ensued around my case. Steve was a very violent man that wanted me dead for burning down his dream house. The police, knowing this, put me on what's called the "county shuffle," moving me from jail to jail every couple of weeks and only bringing me back to Cerro Gordo County on the day of court appearances. During this time, Steve's sister got busted stashing a stockpile of illegal weapons for her brother at her Mason City home (all of this was published in the Mason City Globe-Gazette, for my critics that think I'm just inventing comic book stories out of my previous case). Steve himself was busted for drug-dealing on a large scale.

After his arrest, Steve snitched on 18 other dealers across four other states, and when the feds seized his property, it included a Harley-Davidson shop, a jewelry store and land in Mexico (also printed in the Globe-Gazette). What wasn't printed was how Steve had a 20 thousand dollar contract out on my life, or how the feds tried to get me to help them out in their case against Steve by attempting to get me to agree to a completely fabricated story. I said no thanks to being a snitch, and in turn they ensured that I received the maximum sentence of 10 years in my case, for harming no life; as a first-time felon, I spent 4 years in prison. Most of that time in Anamosa, Iowa, a maximum security penitentiary built in the 1800s and surrounded by 40 foot walls.

I am now facing three federal counts of arson involving animal enterprises across two states, and despite it all I remain in relatively good spirits and as defiant as ever. While arrest and imprisonment are never desirable to the individual or movement, and I definitely have made my mistakes, namely confiding in my brother who fed me to the ATF for pocket change. But show me any imprisoned activist and I'll show you mistakes made. That is why we are, or were, jailed (excluding the rare political set up and growing number of conspiracy cases).

There is an old adage that goes, "If you can't stand the heat, then stay out of the kitchen." It applies well to the underground for Animal Liberation. Activists in other countries seem to understand this far better than we pampered Americans. If you read prison letters from Animal Rights activists like Mel Broughton, Heather Nicholson, Gerrah Selby, Natasha and Greg Avery or Adrian Magdaleno, you will see reflected in their writings and mine a primary concern for Animal and Earth Liberation and acceptance of our fate as prisoners as par for the course. That is a healthy attitude.

We are the landmarks on the road to victory and there will be many more of us before our Mother Earth and her Animal Nations are released from the mechanized oppression of our species. That being said, prison is obviously an unpleasant situation. I would love to be outside enjoying the fresh air in autumn, which is my favorite time of year. But I'm not, because ultimately I choose to resist death and suffering for those that cannot defend themselves. I choose to do so in a clandestine manner and when the hammer of injustice falls down upon my head, it will ultimately be because I decided to act directly and put myself in harm's way.

That's the way the Vegan cookie crumbles, and there is no regrets to be had, no apologies to make. At the bottom of my heart, I care for the plight of Animals and the Earth. I know I can't single-handedly change things, the hell that our kind inflicts on all kinds is bigger than any one person can fix; but I know what I can do. I can fight against it. I can speak out. I can reject abject cruelty in my day-to-day life. I can realize that even though the system seeks my incarceration and cowards spread rumors about me online, that only I can make the decision to be reactive and fearful or revolutionary and unapologetic.

I love my life and I believe in what I say. Adversity, for me, does not change that, it only tests it. This oppressive system wants you to feel as though you've lost before you've begun. It wants us to be reactive and unsure. This system wants us all to be dependent and frightened. They want us divided over a million inconsequential political, religious and personal issues. They want us to seek validation from groups and organizations instead of acting alone. They want these things from us to better control the masses and continue with business as usual. They spend incredible amounts of time, money and effort to ensure and enforce this apathetic and oppressed mentality. **Because the truth is scary. That truth is that one person or a small group of people that are empowered, focused, and courageous can make great changes.** Indeed, it's the only thing that ever does.

The struggle for liberation is not about the individual, even more so for the Animal Rights and Earth Rights camps. It is not who we are, or the hardships we face as activists that are ultimately important. What is important is that we take every opportunity to further the cause, the Animals' cause. That we **remain vital and even and especially in the face of adversity because that's when it counts the most, fair weather activism only goes so far.**

When events radically change in our own life, we need to exhibit enough versatility and integrity to not only weather the storm but embrace opportunity where others see only hardship. As I said in the beginning of this essay, it takes a stout heart. But there is no great reward that does not involve risk. There must at some point be a counterbalance; that is what the radical wing of any movement strives for. **Incredible malice demands incredible compassion.** The cure for greed is selflessness, and the death, torture and abuses that other-than-human Animals endure in secret behind walls, intentionally outside of the sight of the masses, demands outspokenness.

My heart goes out to every person that has sacrificed their freedom for Earth and Animal Liberation. I hope your time is well-spent and you come out of all your trials and tribulations stronger and better off.

For all those who have fought for the entire Earth's fate… Animal liberation whatever it may take!

Animal Liberation: Abolition

I am an Abolitionist Animal Liberation activist and you should be too. How many more Animals have to die before we stop being concerned with 'The Big Picture.' 100 billion? A trillion? How much more of our Mother Earth must be decimated and clear-cut before we draw a line in the sand or forest, as the case may be. I am not a scholar or politician. I am and always have been a street activist. You know, the street. That's where real revolutions are fought, not the halls of academia, where long after the smoke clears, will always pretend to have won what others fought, bled and died for. What I see creeping into the Animal Rights community here in America is a lot of exalted cowardice. That's not to say that there aren't a lot of amazing and selfless folks doing a lot of much needed work on behalf of Animals. There most definitely is. However, as Veganism has grown, so have the cling-ons and posers that think because they are on a Vegan diet they know far more than they do about activism. I hate to rain on the parade, but doing nothing is still doing nothing.

I support Veganism 100% because when everyone follows it strictly, it will be the end of Animal use and abuse. That means it is fundamentally true, because its application is universally good for all. Personally, whether we argue that Veganism has a profound effect or none at all, I adhere to it because I do not want to partake in the worst, deliberate holocaust of innocent life in the history of the planet. That's called doing what's right simply because it's the right thing to do. That being said, my Veganism isn't saving 90 or more Animal lives every year. The world's population is not static, it's growing. On the day you or I go Vegan, 100,000 kids get weaned into eating flesh as food. That is why it is ridiculous to sit around and eat Vegan brownies and act as though you are saving the world.

The true Abolitionist Animal Liberation activist is the person that not only confronts slavery and death in their own consumerism but also opposes it in the world around them. For Abolitionists of every era before us, this has translated into being courageous, resisting the system, and accepting the consequences. Let's look at these one at a time.

Being Courageous

By courage I mean not succumbing to fear when the task at hand demands it. A simple and casual example of this is simply saying what an Animal in a cage would want you to say. Far too often I have seen 'activists' fall into this "you have to meet people where they are" school of thought. No you don't! How people react to the truth is not your responsibility. You cannot always challenge the status quo and be seen as part of it, all at the same time. The belief that Animals exist for their own purposes and not human ends is diametrically opposed to current industrial society. A more extreme example of courage would be putting yourself directly in harm's way for Animals by opposing their oppressors. For example, in a home demonstration where cops and confrontation are bound to ensue, I would rather have one courageous and caring activist by my side that is willing to put her back into her beliefs than 50 cowards that like to play games with words and talk of 'The Big Picture' or the 'long term goals of our movement!' Animals are suffering and dying now. So we should be confronting and saving their lives now; it's not very complicated. In order to be bold and unafraid, it helps to learn to internalize the message. One trait of a coward is that their number one priority is their own absolute safety and comfort. Any tactic that threatens that is always reflexively seen as wrong no matter how effective it obviously is. Look at it this way, if it was you on the chopping block, would you want someone to act on your behalf or have a really interesting philosophical conversation about your impending doom and how we're gonna reform the way it's done by the year 2045. Cowardice is not a virtue and courage is no vice.

Resisting the System and Accepting the Consequences

When you fight the system it is going to fight back. Depending on how effective you are, the oppressor determines the degree to which they will retaliate. By accepting consequences, I do not mean accepting government repression. What I am saying is expect resistance. No matter how 'well within your rights' you are, or 'opposed to illegal activity' you may be, you don't decide the resistance you will meet. Some cop, fed or agent does and they are nothing more than security guards for private corporate interests. In a consumer society you have the right to purchase things and shut up. Conversely, the only true crime is messing with business as usual. When you brace yourself for government, state, or county chicanery, the element of surprise is gone and that is a powerful tool to take out of their hands. To a certain extent it is a compliment. If the security forces of Animal exploitation think well of us then we should think worse of ourselves.

We cannot stop challenging the system. Until we see the changes occur in our society that we believe in, actions for Animal and Earth Liberation must not only occur, but increase. There is not one all encompassing approach. Animal exploitation is not a single-issue problem, it is hydra-headed and multifarious. It encompasses many species and the Earth that is home to us all. So when I speak of resistance, I am not talking about one tactic or avenue. I am talking about the defiance that keeps our movement vital, energetic and an actual threat to the practice of interspecies slavery and objectification. Whether as writers, street level activists, educators, philosophers, or just Vegans, it's good and necessary to feel the immediacy and urgency of our beliefs and of the Animals' pain and sorrow; without passion, resistance is just another bullword. As Veganism and Animal Rights begins to take root in the public consciousness, it is imperative that the message not get lost.

I am incredibly happy with many of the gains over the last 10 years. Even as a prisoner, I am able to request and receive Vegan food. But as the mainstream grows, so must the grassroots; else it becomes just another market for consumers, growing alongside the standard diet of cruelty but never truly diminishing it. We Abolitionist Animal Liberation activists cannot let advertisers turn Veganism into a group of food-obsessed hypochondriacs, or Animal Rights into the philosophical debate society. These issues that we fight for are a matter of life and death for ourselves and countless others. Let's start treating them with the seriousness they deserve and not like a hip new diet fad.

Animal Liberation, whatever it may take!

X To Whom It May Concern X

I was raised in a household of drug and alcohol abuse. My biological father, Mark Zuehlke, was a Vietnam vet that came back from the war and got heavy into cocaine, amphetamines and outlaw biker gangs. My mother, Minerva Marie Matanzo Domench, was raised in Ford Apache, Bronx and born in Puerto Rico. Their marriage produced three children, me being the youngest. My biological parents divorced when I was 12 months old. Some years later, Mark was sent to federal prison for his involvement in one of the largest cocaine/meth busts in Iowa history. I met him for the first time when I was a young man. I travelled to Yankton, South Dakota to the federal prison and visited Mark there. It is my opinion to this day that he was a deadbeat dad, a liar and a scumbag.

My two full blooded brothers, Guthrie and Trapper, were raised by our biological father and I was raised by our biological mother. It has always been unclear to me why they split us up this way, as it was arranged by my parents out of court In any event, my mother remarried the man who became my adopted father. James Bond married my mother in 1984 at which time he adopted me and my last name was legally changed to Bond. I was in diapers when they began dating and he has been the only father I've ever known.

He, unlike Mark, was a good man. But he was a good man with a bad problem. My father (James Bond) was terribly addicted to alcohol. My parents soon divorced when I was ten years old and my mother and I moved to Denver, Colorado to be near her family. By the ripe old age of 12, I was smoking weed with my mother and doing drugs with my "friends." Although I have my G.E.D. (which I received the last time I was in prison), I never made it past the 8th grade. Going to class was far less interesting than getting wasted. I met other kids like me. Friends with broken homes and druggie parents. Biker kids. Punk rock kids. Nerds, geeks and the throwaways. It was the late 80s and bands like Agnostic Front and Sick of it

All were carving out a new style of music called "Crossover." It was a combo of punk and metal. I fell in love! The aggression and angst were all accompanied with a message. A message I could relate to.

Then I heard Straight Edge music and I was hooked (on the music, and drugs). Here was music that was even tighter, the hooks were more rhythmic and it professed ethics I just knew deep down were right. Bands such as Gorilla Biscuits, Youth of Today and Uniform Choice not only changed my life, they saved my life. By the age of 18, my mom had remarried. While I had an affinity for Straight Edge and the drug-free lifestyle, I refused to go to school or do much of anything - besides play drums for my band "Defiance of Authority" and play hacky sack with my friends. My mother's answer to my behavior was to move away to the Pacific Northwest with husband number 3. At that time, we lived in the mountains of Woodland Park, Colorado. I came home from spending the night at a friend's house to find nothing but furniture marks on the floor. I did not see my mother again for 7 years.

At 18 years old without an education or job, I went back to Iowa to stay with my father. In Iowa I learned to work and work hard. Not only because my father does not tolerate laziness but also because socially, in Iowa, if you are not a hard worker than you are looked down upon. To excel at your work in the Midwest is part of the fabric of your everyday life.

By this time it was well into the 90s and two polar extremes were very apparent in my life. On one hand the Straight Edge scene was huge. A new sound had hit and hit hard. Bands like Earth Crisis, Strife, and Snapcase were leading the way and it was an amazing time to wear an 'X' on your hand. Back then, Straight Edge was more than just a "personal choice." It was seriously attempting to stand against drug culture. On the other hand, I had recently met and started getting to know my brother, Trapper. He was hooked on meth. I had never had a brother before and I loved him with all my heart. I loved him blindly. He would steal from me and I would ignore it. He would lie straight into my face

31

and I would excuse it. My brother was always a master and genius at sensing a person's emotional vulnerability and using it to his maximum advantage. Along with Trapper, nearly everyone I had known from Elementary School was either hooked on meth, dealing it, or both. I was fed up. At this point in my life I had been through so much because of other people's (and my own) drug use that I took drastic measures and attacked the source of all this insanity. The dealers themselves. As most know, I attacked with fire the biggest meth dealer in my town.

The four years I spent in prison was without any support from the Straight Edge scene or anyone else. For purposes of self-preservation, most people that truly did know me distanced themselves, as expected, not wanting to become a target of persecution as well. I worked in the prison laundry room for $1.10 a day. That was the extent of my funds. I was also Vegan at that time and had been for a year before my arrest. Luckily the prison system was just beginning to offer a Vegan diet albeit reluctantly. I got X's and V's tattooed on my hands while incarcerated to pledge myself to the drug free lifestyle forever. As a prisoner, they can take everything from you except what's in your heart and your tattoos.

When I got out of prison I found that the 90s were over. The Edge kids from the 90s that I knew had given it up. Everybody was 'really concerned' about me and 'just about to write a letter.' Suffice it to say, I was pissed off. I distanced myself from the people and the music. For years I was bitter. To me, Straight Edge was very personal, life-changing and serious. Fighting against drug dealers had landed me in prison with a permanent felony record, not to mention more than one fist fight.

As the years went by, Veganism and Animal Liberation became the focus of my life. I tried reconnecting with the younger generation of Straight Edge and teaching them the importance of Veganism and standing up against drug culture. But with most, apathy is king. Apparently, the bulk of the Straight Edge scene is about collecting records and keeping it to yourself. That and politics, politics, politics. Instead of the primary focus being on Animal Liberation or drug-free living, it seems that half of Straight Edge is about being a Christian, Right-wing American Patriot that resemble a bunch of clean-cut cops with tattoos. Bullying people at hardcore shows and staying dedicated to the "boys only" mentality. While the other half are wanna-be Beatnik, Bohemian anarchists that go ten steps out of their way to be offended about everything, but won't do anything except philosophize and try to squeeze the words "patriarchal" and "heteronormative" into as many conversations as possible.

I would prefer to not be so divisive as to demand that everyone adhere to my checklist of political views and believe me, I have them. But idealism and reality are not always going to meet. For instance, I have already met people in county jail whose company I enjoy. People that make me laugh. People with dynamic personalities. I am not going to deny their camaraderie just because we differ. Just like how most Vegans or Straight Edge people are not going to disown their parents for drinking milk or smoking cigarettes.

Presently, I am facing the trials of my life, quite literally. This time I am happy to say that many people from around the world write me often, which brings more joy to my heart than I can express. It's awesome to know that I am not alone. But once again, I feel nothing but scrutiny and unresponsiveness from the Straight Edge community. However, this time I am not in the mood. I will live my life drug-free for the rest of my life and will not 'break edge' as they say. But I am through with "the scene" because it has become a fashion show and politically pretentious joke. My people, my family, my sphere of concern outside of our Mother Earth and her Animal Nations is primarily for those that are moved by Animal Liberation and biocentrism. I have sacrificed my freedom every bit as much for the Straight Edge as I have for Animal Rights. Outside of the best band on the planet (Earth Crisis) making a video about me (which isn't a community supporting me, but the vanguards of it), I have received nothing but bullshit from Straight Edge people, then and now.

I regret fighting so hard for a group of posers and pretentious gossip hounds, my trust isn't free anymore. I will always have respect for those within Straight Edge that use it as a foundation for militant and positive change. The rest of you mean nothing to me.

P.S. My father has been a recovering alcoholic and sober for a decade now and my mom lives in the Alaskan wilderness and is as feral and free as she ever was.

I Am the ALF "Lone Wolf"

On April 30, 2010 at 3:30 am I burned the Sheepskin Factory in Denver, Colorado to the ground. I did so strictly following Animal Liberation Front (ALF) guidelines to harm no life while at the same time maximizing damage to a business of Animal exploitation. I used the nickname "Lone Wolf" in my communications to the media, even though I knew that using such a moniker made my actions easier for the authorities to link together. I did it for a specific reason that I will get to a little later in this article, but for now, let me back up and explain how and why I came to join the Animal Liberation Front.

My start in Animal Rights began about 14 years ago. I would order pamphlets about vivisection, Veganism, factory farms, and other forms of Animal abuse and put them on windshields in parking lots and on community bulletin boards. I was very zealous in wanting to educate people. Having worked building slaughterhouses, I was certain that if everyone knew what I knew they would all become Vegan. After about a year of such flyering, I ended up having my activism interrupted with a prison sentence for arson (that crime was not Animal Rights-related, but also harmed no living being). During the 4 years of my incarceration, I studied Animal Rights, biocentrism, philosophy, world history, evolution, religion, mythology, law, social justice movements, politics, sociology; anything I could get my hands on that was non-fiction. Some people go to Penn State, I got my education at the State Pen.

In any event, upon my release from prison and completion of parole, I moved back to Denver, Colorado, the city where I had spent my teenage years. I had a couple of close friends still kicking around the north suburbs, and also had an aunt and some cousins there. By this time, it was 2003. I had by now surmised that it wasn't a lack of education that allowed cruelty to Animals to continue, because Animal

Rights activists had uncovered and publicized so much video evidence of profound evil in vivisection labs, slaughterhouses, and entertainment over the last three decades that the gore would gag a maggot. Nor was it a problem of disseminating this information; with the meteoric rise of the internet, anyone who wanted to know what happened to their "meal" could find out at the push of a button and click of the mouse.

I had talked with enough people by this point to see that deep down inside not everyone is a caring Vegan. Lots of people don't care at all for Animals, they just have cat and dog fetishes, or they care right up to the point where you ask them to stop eating the dead carcasses of murdered Animals. I found many people far more outraged at the fact that I was bringing the issues up than at the issues themselves. Apparently, if you support death and slavery three times a day, that's not a problem, but if I point that fact out, then I'm the asshole. I decided to turn my attention to the Animals themselves.

Much of that period of time I cannot detail, since saving Animals from death and torture is considered terrorism by the United States government. But I will say this: when you take the risk to save an Animal from a horrible death and look into their eyes and see the gratitude and love, it changes you. On that day you become a better person and you once again know right from wrong with child-like simplicity.

Eventually, being a social person, I began mingling with the local Vegan community. I was invited to a local meet-up, where I immediately felt out of place. The local Denver Vegan community had about as much diversity in it as a Ku Klux Klan rally. I had been working part-time with an Abolition Animal Rights organization whose main focus were the promotion of Veganism and speaking out for farm animals, especially so-called "free range" and "cage free." As the night wore on, many of the trust fund-afarian and hippie-crits started to let their high and mighty opinions fly, due to the ridiculous amounts of that beer they were ingesting. What ensued next was akin to some creepy form of speed-dating where everyone went around in a circle and very briefly introduced themselves, named their occupation, and told what they did for Animals. Never before or since have I witnessed such intellectual egoism.

When it was my turn, I mentioned my stand against "free range," I was met instantly with eye rolls and rationalizations about it being "a step in the right direction" and "Rome wasn't built in a day," even, "I'm Vegan but I am so glad that meat-eaters now have a humane and cruelty-free alternative!" My response was, "I can't believe I am listening to a group of Vegans promoting animal use!" After this, a huge argument ensued and I left that meet-up determined to expose "free range" and once again educate everyone I could. Only this time with more zeal and vigor than ever.

I began flyering all over Denver about "free range" – thousands of windshields all throughout downtown. I would flyer until my thumb and fingers were blistered from lifting windshield wipers. I tabled at events and talked with hundreds of people. I went to punk and hardcore concerts and tried to recruit the youth. I began laying the groundwork for a group I called V.F.L. (Vegan For Life); in short, I did everything in my power to motivate and promote Animal Liberation, even at work. I was a bulk foods manager for a local health food store. I got "VEGAN" tattooed across my throat and talked with any customer that would approach me about it, which was a lot of people in and of itself.

For a while, I had a blog where I wrote articles and sought to revive and revise the Vegan Hardline philosophy. However, the more I did, the more my frustration grew. People that I talked to at tabling events would listen to all I had to say about dairy cows being raped for their milk, their calves being turned into veal, then the cows themselves being turned into burgers and leather. People would stare back at me blankly and respond, "Man, I couldn't give up cheese, dude. Cheese is so good." I would go back to areas I had flyered, only to find half the flyers on the ground.

All the punk rock kids thought it was okay to eat meat as long as it was out of a dumpster, and the hardcore and

Straight Edge kids were more into practicing dance moves and playing video games than putting their back into their beliefs. I became burnt out.

The few friends I had liked to talk about how righteous we were for being Vegan and how wrong the rest of the world was, blah, blah, blah. I became as annoyed with pretentious Vegans as I was with anyone else. For a few months, all I did was work. I was depressed because I felt marginalized and ineffective; I began daydreaming at work about what I would do if I had no fear, nothing to lose. I would be a member of that clandestine underground, I would be an Animal Liberation Front operative. The more I thought about it, the happier I became. Then one day while stalking the potato chip isle at work, it hit me: there's no time like the present. I quit my job and left my normal life in isle seven of a health food store.

The first thing I knew was that I would work alone. I had known and been around many different local activists and there was not one of them I would have considered up to the challenge. The next thing I knew was that I wanted to go big. With the current government crackdown on any kind of effective Animal Rights campaign, I might as well go for it. If they're gonna try to catch me and call me a terrorist for breaking a McDonald's window, I might as well think much bigger.

I picked the Sheepskin Factory in Denver for two reasons. Primarily because they make a lot of money selling pelts and fur, Animals suffer and die so that people can have a fuzzy steering wheel or a soft cushion on a motorcycle seat. In my opinion, they are no better than the Nazis that made hobbycraft items out of Jews. Secondly, the place just looked flammable. I will never divulge how I did it because it's not important; where there's a will, there's a way.

After it was all said and done, I felt great! I had destroyed an Animal exploitation facility and I had cost the Animal industry over half a million dollars. I used the name "ALF Lone Wolf" in the media to convey to my ALF brothers and sisters worldwide (whoever they are) the power of acting alone. I wanted anyone that cares to know that one person can accomplish a lot. Unfortunately, I was apprehended because of an informant; my deepest regret is that I confided in this one person. But still the principle stands; all I was tricked into doing was telling on myself and my entire 3-month campaign cost me 150 bucks, and cost Animal abusers three-quarters of a million dollars.

On February 11, 2011 I will be sentenced. Whatever sentence is imposed will only be a third of my tribulations; I still have to face charges in Utah. The US Attorneys want people to think that the Animal Liberation Front, and me in particular, are terrorists. I am not a terrorist, and the ALF is not a terrorist organization; actually, it's not even an organization. The ALF is any Vegan or vegetarian that harms no life and decides by illegal means to liberate Animals and/ or cause economic damage to those that profit from Animal use and abuse. Since our inception in 1976, no Animal or human has been harmed; quite the opposite. Thousands of lives have been saved and thousands of Animal abusers have been stopped. A terrorist is a person or group that targets and kills innocent beings to create panic and control by fear.

On April 30th, 3:30 in the morning, my life changed. I got sick of seeing industries of death continue unchallenged and I decided to do something drastic about it. I am proud that I had the courage to act on behalf of those that cannot defend themselves. I can look deep into my heart know that I did not fail them and I did all that I could; and believe me, when you live in a cage that's all you wish for someone to do.

Animal Liberation, whatever it may take!

Biocentric and Symbiotic

I contend that you cannot truly be for Animal Liberation without having at least an equal concern for Earth Liberation. The primary reason for this is because all life is symbiotic with its environment. As adults in contemporary Western Eurocentric society we are taught to compartmentalize everything we see. This stems from a maniacal urge to relate everything strictly in terms of personal worth. In other words, we are taught from day one to view the world solely from our point of view: human centric and human supreme.

One interesting way you can view human supremacy at work in almost anyone is to ask the question "Tell me about World History." Practically every person I have ever asked that question to has reflexively answered with examples of human history only from various times and places. Seldom will you hear about the history of the dinosaurs, the tectonic movements of continents, or the profound abundance and evolution of aquatic life. Nor will you hear about the endless species, types and abundance of the plant kingdom or the movements and cycles of Mother Earth herself. No. Usually if someone really digs deep you may hear about hominids or our next of kin, apes. Which apparently are only important because of their close relation to us.

Looking at nearly all the World religions we see similarly that the god or gods of all creation are just smitten with us humans. In the Holy Bible, there is barely two pages in the beginning of Genesis explaining the creation of the entire material universe, the Earth and all its critters. The rest is all about people. How ridiculously vain to think that all life is only here for the benefit of one life. In Hindu mythology we find that for some unexplained reason humans are at the top of the Karmic food chain and to be born human is one step away from divinity. I assert that it is these kinds of utterly insatiable vanities that have made humans a cancer and pestilence to the Earth and all life upon her. I think that one can definitely be spiritual and still separate from such profound speciesist, self-centeredness. Atheists, although much more free-thinking in many ways, seem to carry all the vestiges of human supremacy as well. Even U.F.O.-ologists assume that aliens - which are always depicted as humanoid - would be brilliant enough to warp time and space to travel the multiverse just so that they could come here to Earth and insert cold, metallic objects into our rectums. Real, rational way to think it through.

Anyway, back to what matters - the Earth. As I said, we are not important, Mother Earth is. And all life is 100% dependent on her 100% of the time. Without oxygen to breath, you would die in a matter of minutes. Without water, a matter of days. Without food, a matter of months. And without a natural environment, a matter of years. Mother Nature is the real goddess and we are just a tiny entry in her book of Life. The only thing that makes us important, really, is our profound wickedness and evil on the face of the globe.

Many times in my writings I refer to Animal and Earth death as a "holocaust." I realize that people being human-centric view 'The Holocaust' as the worst thing that ever happened. But truthfully that is a drop in the bucket compared to our own holocaust against the Earth. What happened to the Jews at the hands of the Nazis was insane and cruel. What whites have done to the Native peoples and still do to them all over the globe is atrocious. But while of course there are correlations to be made amongst all forms of oppression, these are not really comparisons. What one segment of the human race does to another is nowhere near the perfidiousness of our species against all other species. We (humanity) destroy, lay waste and make extinct whole species and varieties of Life. We hunt them to death, eat them to death and poach them to death. We cut down their habitats and poison the bio-dome. We perpetuate the biggest holocaust ever in the history of the world! We domesticate, subjugate and seal the fate of all. There is only two ways that this theater of insanity will end. Either we will adopt a biocentric attitude or we will trash the Earth until she retaliates (and guess what, our collective grey brain matter is not going to win against the fury of the Earth).

Biocentric is just a way of saying from our Mother Earth's point of view instead of just our own species (by 'our' I mean all Life not just humans). To begin the paradigm shift to a biocentric worldview is a life-long journey for us alienated humans. We are the original domesticated animal. The first step is interconnectedness. As I said earlier, all Life is symbiotic to its surroundings or environment. There are millions of examples of this in nature. One simple one is a squirrel on a tree. It's obvious to me that they are extensions of one another. A squirrel is roughly the same color as the tree bark. Its little feet and claws perfectly adapted to climb as ours are to the ground. Conversely, the tree perfectly sustains the squirrel with sustenance and shelter. And the squirrel keeps predators away and spreads the seed for the tree. Symbiotic. And equally simple but a more curious mystery of interconnectedness is 'the face.' Nearly all Life has a face. Under water, on land, in the air. Eyes, ears, nose, mouth. Why? Because all Life on Mother Earth is a manifestation of the intelligence of nature, far more majestic and imaginative than any one of the entries in her book of Life.

Just as there are millions of ways in which we can observe the symbiotic relationships between Earth and Animal, there are just as many ways we can ponder on interconnectedness. Far too many for this brief article. But none of these contemplations matter unless they manifest themselves in our actions. If our understanding of connectivity doesn't change our behaviors then we really do not understand it to begin with. When I first went Vegan, I remember feeling a certain power about it. Looking back, I now know that what I felt was a little bit of integration. A step towards being a part of things, instead of trying to be supreme. I can eat animals and their by-products if I choose to. That is my ability. But I don't feel that it is my right. Just because I can, doesn't mean that I should.

Taking myself out of that perceived position - namely

being part of a "superior race," the human race - alleviated a splinter in my mind. It helped me in my dealings with others and it helped me stand up and fight for those that cannot fight for themselves. The interconnected mentality still helps me today. My petty fears and tribulations are not what is important; I am not important. What I am a part of is important. What I fight for is important. This Earth is my Mother and you owe your Mother your life. The animals that live all around us, great and small, are other Nations, fellow sentients as we are. Not just with their own species characteristics but individuals as well. Just as no two people, cats, or dogs are alike.

The only thing we do better than the rest is manipulate our surroundings. We warp, bend, and alchemize until we have cars, phones, bombs and whatever we envision. But we use our nature-given abilities for selfish ends and to the Earth's detriment. Our advancement seems to be the Earth's cancer. There are at least a dozen insects I can think of off the top of my head that are vital to the ecosystem. But if we humans ceased to exist immediately, we wouldn't be missed. The Earth would be far better off.

Since I am biocentric, I am not a fan of technologically advanced civilization. The more we innovate, the more people compartmentalize. In the process, people turn into social invalids. Instead of talking to the person next to you on the bus, you sit there frigid and text a person on the other side of town. Instead of engaging in real social interactions, we become part of 'online communities' where everyone is only what they portray and nobody else's foibles need to be dealt with or even admitted. Instead of confronting evil, we blog about it, as if everyone's sheepish agreement to an ideology could ever take the place of doing something about it. I would rather fist fight a fascist than 'friend' a bunch of armchair generals. The more we philosophize and make these issues abstract, the further away we get from doing something about it.

The solution to the Earth being murdered isn't to wear skinny jeans and not bathe. The solution is the same as when

Native Americans trod the warpath for our Mother Earth. It's the same as when the Black Panther Party became sick of watching cops kill their people in the streets. And it's the same as when the Suffragettes got sick of being beaten with the same 'rule of thumb' that the great-grandparents of the Black Panthers were whipped to pieces under. That solution is to see the problems for what they are, refuse to accept them any longer, and fight like hell until you're dead, imprisoned, or things change! That is the reality. You do not 're-wild' by being domesticated.

Our Mother Earth does not need spokespersons, she needs warriors. If these words seem severe, it only because something must counteract the cowardice and apathy of the First World, consumer junkie drones. The militant Animal Liberation movements and the militant Earth Liberation movements are extensions of one another. Just as the squirrel and the tree. Together we form the pinnacle of all other liberation movements because if we fail there will be no more humanity to liberate. The time will soon be upon us where our Mother Earth will retaliate just as a body seeks to destroy a virus and the upheaval will affect the just and unjust alike. And no matter what we believe, we will pay for having not acted.

Earth Liberation, whatever it may take!

Revolutionary and Militant

Two buzzwords I often hear in various radical circles are "revolutionary" and "militant." I think they are two very important words that have become far too commonly used and thus do not command the respect they deserve. In this essay, I am going to put a fresh perspective on the word "revolutionary" and get back to the definition of "militant." All this from the perspective and for the benefit of the Abolitionist Animal Liberation activists and radical environmentalists that care more about our Mother Earth and her Animal Nations than contemporary industrialized society.

Revolutionary

Advertisers would like us to think that their products are revolutionary. Politicians would have us think that revolutionaries are "radical" and "extreme." Religionists believe their prophets to be standard-bearers of revolution. I guess the common usage for "revolutionary" might mean anything that brings about great change, and in particular, great change for the cause or causes in which one believes. But for me, the importance is in "How do we effect great change?" Therefore, I view revolutionary as a steadiness instead of an event horizon. From my unorthodox view of the word, I find a planet in orbit to be the best and most accurate depiction.

A planet in orbit stays in orbit. Revolution after revolution, our Mother Earth stays that course of action. No matter what obstacles fall in the path of travel, be it asteroids or comets. Even if a confrontation with another planet were to occur, threatening the certain deaths of both planets, our Mother Earth would not move. Even though, to an outside observer, the failure to move out of the way or change direction may seem suicidal, or the inability to budge may seem to be unreasonable. In any case, the Earth can only remain in orbit. She revolves, she is revolutionary.

But what if that were not the case? What if our Mother

Earth were reactionary? Every time an asteroid was on a crash course, she moved. Same for comets and any other obstacles. Soon these deviations in course would add up; eventually the gravity from the Sun wouldn't be strong enough to aptly apply and not only would the orbit or course be compromised, but life on the planet's surface would end and there would remain no useful movements within the Earth's actions.

Back to the Animal and Earth Lib movements
The same rule of revolutionary movement applies to Earth and Animal Liberation.

We as Abolitionists are the ones that continue upon a straightforward path toward our goals. This is of incredible import because there are many other forces trying to divert us from reaching the event horizon of change. Because if or when it occurs, it means the end of property being more important than life. That is a serious problem for those that profit off the death and subjugation of the sentient. So we fight for the total freedom of Animals. We do this in any approach we take. We do not protest "how" KFC kills chickens; we protest "that" KFC kills chickens. We don't promote vegetarianism, because trading in solid flesh for liquid flesh is no gain.
Most Animal exploitation industries are connected, therefore supporting one is supporting all.

Example
A dairy cow, like any other mammal, only lactates when she is pregnant. Therefore, she is artificially inseminated against her will; another way to say this is that she is raped. This keeps her milk production high; every time production falls, she is raped again. Her children become veal calves confined so thoroughly that any movement, even standing, is made all but impossible. At the end of her miserable life, after she has been repeatedly raped and her children all killed and when she can no longer produce enough to satisfy her "owner" under even forced circumstances, she gets turned into burgers and leather.

Go Vegan!
As true Abolitionist Animal Liberation activists, we do not value property or business over life.

Welfarists, on the other hand, are reactionary
Being truly reactionary, the welfare arm of Animal Rights seems to have no definitive goals outside of lobbying for such things as four more inches of cage space that two more chickens will get put into, or having sit downs with ranchers to let the rest of us know they are "really nice people, just like you and me." Just like you and me, except that they kill for a living and seek to kill more and profit more year after bloody year. In a lot of my run-ins with welfarists, I have noticed a few absorb core beliefs that don't make any logical sense.

First, they all seem to believe that if people think you are nice, they will just radically change their lives to be just like you.

Second, they seem to think almost anything is a victory for Animals, things such as a car honking at you when you hold a sign in your hands at a protest. While I agree moral support feels good, I'm fairly certain that if every horn in every car on Earth blew at this very moment in solidarity with Animals, it wouldn't so much as save one life.

Third, welfarists have no sense of urgency; stopping Animal exploitation now is an impossible dream for them. Instead, they look to a grand future where somehow the war for Earth and Animals is won because we were all really nice and morally superior for a couple of generations. (Of course, when it comes to needing money, there is a huge sense of urgency and victory is just 1500 bucks away.)

And lastly, respect for authority and law is promoted with religious zeal, to the point where many of these welfarists would have turned me in to the feds as quickly as my own brother and for probably half the money.

In the end, welfarism works hand in glove with many Animal exploitation industries. Instead of standing firm on a platform of non-use of Animals, these reactionaries have brought us "free range," "cage free," "humane slaughter" and a bunch of other nice-sounding terms to appease everyone and change nothing. And therein lies the danger.

Our revolutionary movement cannot compete with the lobby power of corporate Animal and Earth killers. That's not to say that Abolition doesn't belong in politics; it most certainly does. What it does say is that we must be aware of how to navigate a playing field that is bought and paid for by corporate devils. Our first priority now and forever shall be to save Animal lives and the biosphere, without which there is no life. Our second priority is to speak truth. As long as an Animal in a cage seeks total freedom, then we seek their total freedom. Lastly, our third priority is to educate the public about the positive effects of Veganism and the various plights of Animals. At this stage of Earth use and abuse, all else is hobbyism and human-centered bullshit.

Militant

The word usually invokes thoughts of the military, or adherence to a strict discipline. But as I look the word up in a dictionary, the definition of the word militant is: adj. 1A: engaged in warfare B. prone to fighting 2. aggressively active, especially in a cause. I can think of no better word to describe what we all should aspire to as Abolitionist Animal Liberation activists.

Engaged in warfare

A cursory glance will reveal that there is a war, mainly a lopsided war where humans and our supremacist mentality are raping the Earth and causing more torture and pain to every critter in our way than our limited minds can comprehend. Yes, there is a war and we should all be engaged in the fight to defend all innocent life.

Prone to fighting

There are many ways to fight. You can fight with your fist, with your mind, with your tenacity. The ways in which you can fight are limited only by your imagination. But there can be no fight without confrontation. In this day and age we are all programmed not to confront anything. Practice speaking truth instead of biting your tongue. Of course, there are times to use tact (I wouldn't go to dinner and call my grandmother a flesh-eating bastard), but as a central rule when protesting, tabling or otherwise on the clock for Animal Rights, if you don't have anything nice to say, then don't say anything nice.

Aggressively active in our cause
We all have different abilities and talents. Do an honest self-assessment, learn what your strongest attributes are and employ them to this most important of all struggles, mainly biocentrism and the total freedom of the Animal Nations from human use and abuse. Like a planet in orbit, accept no obstacle and remember: whether you live to see the end to this tyranny is not what's important, but rather that we spend our lives earnestly fighting for it.

Animal Liberation, whatever it may take!

Slaughterhouse Blues (Why I am Vegan Part II)

Hogs have been genetically tampered with for so long that we no longer know many of their natural attributes. We do know that in nature no hog is pink. That is a genetic modification because people like "light colored pork." We also know that no hog in the wild gets up to 800 pounds which is a ridiculously obese size. Many times when I worked at IBP (Iowa Beef Producers, which is the largest producer of "pork" in the midwest and I am fairly certain in the nation) I would see hogs that were so unnaturally overweight that one or all of their limbs were crushed under the weight. In this essay I am going to go back to that chamber of horrors to better detail the suffering that thinking, feeling and sentient beings we know as pigs endure at the hands of speciesist human oppressors.

Early in the morning it starts, semi-loads of doomed pigs arrive at the slaughterhouse. They are packed in "assholes to elbows" as the drivers so succinctly put it. At least three hogs per truck will be deemed "unfit for human consumption" usually due to huge abscesses on their hind legs. This happens because a few hogs per trailer always get their rears stuck against the air hole grating. When this happens their hindquarters become horrifically blistered from a 30 hour ride in this condition. Imagine sitting on a school bus with no pants and a cheese grater for a seat. Upon arrival an IBP supervisor inspects the hogs. Any hogs that absolutely cannot be "used" get thrown out behind the facility to either die of exposure or to starve to death. It's not uncommon to see drivers or IBP supervisors stabbing hogs in the hind legs with pocket knives to pop abscesses and continue with business as usual. The hogs then get filtered from the back of the trailers to the pen runs. This is a very temporary holding area where they wait to be killed. On the opposite side from the trailer docking is the "shoot." All the hogs get forced into this single file death run made of tubular steel. Once inside the shoot they are on a death march, they cannot turn around and because of the

54

steady flow of their doomed brethren being forced in behind them, they cannot stop. Hogs have the cognitive ability of a 5 year old child. They are very smart and very aware what's happening. They tremor from fear, some are so frightened they lose control of their bodily functions. Others faint and get pushed along their bellies to death. In any event, there is no stopping.

The impending horror is imminent. Once at the top of the shoot there is an abrupt 45 degree ramp. At the top of which an electrified bolt thrusts out and jolts the hog in the head to knock them out. They then land unconscious, or awake and paralyzed on the conveyor belt. Here they meet the "sticker." The sticker has the job of stabbing the hogs in the throat and shackling their hind leg so that they bleed to death while hanging upside down. At the IBP plant in Perry, Iowa the stickers wear hockey masks so that if a hog regains consciousness prematurely and kicks them in the face, they will be protected. Can you imagine being hung upside down by a lunatic in a hockey mask and having your throat cut! So much for your welfarist "humane slaughter!" Very quickly they awaken gushing blood from the throat, traveling upside down in a corridor of congealing blood. The floor beneath is pitched at a 45 degree angle so that much of the blood drains into the blood tanks one level beneath the kill floor in a department called rendering. As they awaken they begin kicking and panicking. This is good according to industry standards because it quickens the bleed out. At the pinnacle of this A-frame shackle drive, the slow ride is over. They slide along the shackle channel very fast, approximately 35 ft descent and 40 ft in length. Because of this acute slide angle approximately one in every one hundred hogs fall from the shackle and end up on the floor beneath. There they stay drenched in the blood that rains down from the "sliders" above. Every shift change the line stops just long enough to power-spray the "jelly" off of the "fallers" and shackle them back up for "production," on the kill floor.

Hopefully by the time they reach this point they are

dead, but that is not always the case. The first machine is the "beater." This machine is much like the rollers of a car wash except they rollers have thick nylon ropes with knots on the ends. This machine beats the hair off the hogs. Next is 'the washer.' This is a long scalding hot water bath/basin. This gets the residual hair that the "beater" missed and softens the skin for "disassembly." From this point everything works at a "break neck pace" (a term coined by the slaughterhouse industry in reference to the speed with which the kill floor operates). The head and hoofs are chopped off. The flesh peeled, salted, and stacked on pallets to be shipped to a leather tanning facility. The ribs sawed and broken and the innards dumped into stainless steel trays traveling along a conveyor belt to rendering with the blood tanks, bone cages and other waste bins. Every slaughterhouse has a section or sometimes separate facility on the same property called "rendering." A more accurate description would be "junkyard of death." Blood tanks, bone bins, 40 gallon drums of eyeballs, etc. The slaughterhouse industry is in cahoots with many, many food producers to hide their death junk in various foods. Many mass produced breads have powdered bones in the mix. Gelatins and lards get shoved into everything from cupcakes and Twinkies to car and truck tires. Blood gets used for rennet, an adhesive and oddly enough an ingredient in cheese (Sorry vegetarians but your cheese is not vegetarian. It's a combination of lactation and blood). And on and on.

It must be said that rendering is such a disgusting and wretched mess that few can stand it. I once had to work welding a blood tank and the smells were so intense, I spent the four hours it took to complete the task vomiting in a bucket, much to the amusement of the workers. I wish I could more accurately portray the evil and insanity of an IBP plant. But I can't. Words and videos only tell a small truth of the filth and misery. I can't describe the smells, the screams, or the terror that these Animals experience. So often Animal Rights Activists will get hung up on one detail or part of the kill process but I will tell you it's sick and wrong from start to finish! I will say this as well, it's not intentionally cruel. This is the way it must be done to feed several million people several billion Animals. It's unreasonable to ask that people that kill Animals all day long as fast as technologically possible to also care about the Animals at the same time. No! The answer is to GO VEGAN and destroy the death camps, raze them to the ground just as if they were Auschwitz or Dachau! Because that is what they are, concentration camps to the hundredth power!

But before my anger carries me away let's return to the slaughterhouse so I can explain the human oppression as well. The grunt workers, the ones that deal with all the gore, filth and danger are known as the "white hats" (In IBP, your place in the hierarchy is worn on your head with the color of your hard hat, denoting your rank). The white hats were all African immigrants except for the clean-up crews which were all Latino immigrants. The white hats run the kill floor, rendering and stacking and salting skins. They are paid the bare minimum and allowed no leeway whatsoever. They work 12 hour shifts with a 20 minute lunch and two 10 minute breaks. They are constantly threatened with write-ups for the slightest deviation from the rules or slow down in production. Three write-ups within six months and they're fired, turned into immigration and deported. Approximately 1 out of 5 white hats is missing a finger or part of their finger from working at ridiculously frantic pace with pneumatic scissors and saws.

The white hats' direct supervisors are the "yellow hats." There are three yellow hats in every area of the facility with the exception of the kill floor which has five. Every yellow hat I ever saw was an extremely angry 30-40ish white male, whose main job seemed to be to ridicule and frighten the white hats. I was a "blue hat" which meant I was a construction worker for an independent contractor, not to be confused with IBP maintenance men which wore "red hats." I had full run on the facility and was allowed to be anywhere at any time. That kind of freedom angered the yellow hats. More than once I had to explain to a yellow hat that my work was none of his business and to stay out of my way. The yellow hats bosses are the "green hats." The green hats are rarely seen on the floor unless the USDA are present or production has stopped for any reason. The USDA were known as the "white coats" due to their white smocks. Now, the USDA has real power. They can shut down a facility without notice at any time and for any length of time. For this reason everyone is nervous when the white coats are around. But as I said the demand for meat is huge. Quotas to suppliers cannot be met if a facility were to close for even 24 hours. Anybody that works in a slaughterhouse sees so many health violations occur in a day that you couldn't keep count of them all if you tried. The white coats know this, so the way it goes is no surprise. Literally, no surprise visits. Three days before a USDA inspector visits, the slaughterhouse is alerted. A massive cleanup is initiated on the day of inspection. The white coats walk from one end of the plant to the other with their face buried in a clipboard and flanked on either side by green hats. The kill line is temporarily slowed down while they're in the building. The whole inspection takes about a half hour. Before the USDA can even leave the parking lot, it's back to the break-neck pace and filthy gore.

Long after I left that hideous facility in Perry, Iowa and went Vegan, I found myself wondering why do we as a "civilized" society allow this to happen? Why did I not personally intervene when I had the chance? Why did it take me several years after bearing witness to this atrocity to seriously begin speaking out and fighting against it? The answer to all these questions is one word: speciesism. We, humanity, feel that we are inherently better and more important than all other forms of life put together. So completely do we believe this that even many of those that are Vegan and Animal Rights activists have yet to contend fully with their own speciesism. For if we had a real sense of the evil wrought against Animals that people call "food," the movement for their liberation would be far more voracious and militant than it is now. Instead of consoling each other with how much we "feel their pain" (which we don't) or simply falling apart at the seams whenever viewing or even thinking about their plight (which helps a doomed Animal about as much as total apathy), we should ante up and do something about it.

The proper response to evil is not fear. The proper response to wickedness is not helplessness. The proper response to callousness is not to weep uncontrollably. The proper response to evil, wickedness and callousness is outrage, confrontation, and action! We need to look deep within ourselves and be honest about how much stronger we would feel about acting against these horrors and insanities if they were happening to people and then bridge that gap in our own speciesism. For on the day that we do we will quit crying all the time for the Animals! And start fighting all the time for the Animals! Our Mother Earth and her Animal Nations need us to be effective not affected. The truth is that we self-professed Animal defenders have a greater knowledge of these atrocities. We also presumably have a higher sensitivity to them. And I assert that we therefore have a greater responsibility to do something about it. To have a greater knowledge about a crime and do nothing about it is in itself, a crime. It is called complicity.

And here's some knowledge. All the Animals that die annually for fur, entertainment, and vivisection globally, those numbers of dead are equaled by the American meat packing industry in one day! Over half of our fresh water, drinking water goes to "livestock!" The number one polluter of our water is the run-off aka shit from farmed animals. The number one culprit of deforestation and displacement of indigenous people is the meat industry! But simply knowing these things doesn't change them. Any more than knowing a recipe is going to feed you.
It's time to liberate, educate and agitate.

Animal Liberation, whatever it may take!

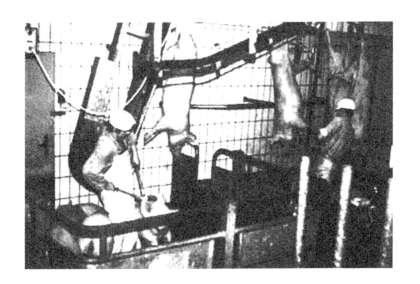

Vegan Wolf Tribe

Well, my sentencing is right around the corner and the last 12 months of my life have been interesting ad tumultuous to say the least. A good friend once told me, "People that live best and are the most well received are those that represent themselves exactly as they are." That has proved to be the most accurate and difficult statement to live up to I have ever heard. Well buddy, "We win again!" Sometimes I've felt like Atlas with the weight of the world on my shoulders. But my supporters have been amazing and your efforts never go unappreciated by me. That said I wish to express my thanks.

First and foremost, to the Animals that have changed my life. To E.T. (Extra Trouble) the most amazing cat I have ever known. To all the hogs I saw die at IBP I am still sorry and disgusted with my own inaction and you will always be my sense of urgency. To the Llama, Carrie that always came running to give me Llama kisses. To Jeffrey Thomas, the best Goat ever. R.I.P to Francis the Sheep that Suzie, Chad and I buried. Thanks for teaching me that what we do is important because life doesn't last. To Lerr the Rooster who went from a cage straight to my lap and taught me that roosters can purr. Thanks to "Walter" the Turkey that was liberated on Thanksgiving week of 2009 because another activist couldn't just take pictures of those sheds without saving one. To the Deer who got away because I unburied those poacher's salt licks and tossed them in the lake. To Reese the Greyhound that went through hell and now only runs when he wants to. And to all those I couldn't save, I'm so sorry I failed you.

As an A.L.F. operative and Direct Activist, I was the "Lone Wolf." I am no longer alone. Many people I have never met have rushed to my aid now that I'm in a cage. Along with a few old friends. It's a curious thing when you become a political prisoner, people you assumed would always have your back can be the first to denounce or distance themselves. And others you would never expect to be are in your corner.

I am learning to not judge people so harshly or trust people so readily. Those people in my life (since my arrest) that have had my best interest at heart have offered me loyalty, ferocity, defense from attack and true love. Whether near or far, you are my Vegan Wolf Tribe.

Huge thanks to Elizabeth for keeping me sane when I'm falling apart at the seams. You are always more concerned with my well being than I am, much love my Vegan sister. Thank you Michele for showing me that women possess an emotional intelligence and intuitiveness that we men do not, but can always learn from. Thanks to everyone in Denver that visits me a half hour a week through busted Plexiglas. Thank you Judith for writing me far more than I am ever able to write back. Thank you to Salt Lake City simply for being Salt Lake City. Love it or leave it. The Support Walter Crew: the best support an activist could ever hope for. To NAALPO for being the most amazing, uncompromising voice of Animal Liberation, bar none!

With that said, I am proud that I've become the first ever imprisoned Press Officer of the North American Animal Liberation Press Office. I assure you it is not a paper title. I have recently been doing interviews with a couple different press outlets. As many of you know, I continue writing essays and will continue to while dealing with court and jail here and in Salt Lake City. And once the final gavel has swung I will begin writing a book or two. As an imprisoned activist I feel a responsibility to set a positive example of continued activism. There is too much of a fear culture within Animal and Earth Liberation movements. Phrases like "Green Scare" really only succeed in conveying the message that we're scared to be green, or that we should be. I cannot accept that, I will not. The proper response to evil and oppression is outrage, not fear. But I do not give orders. I command nothing. Leaderless resistance is the winning model in the legal above ground and clandestine underground. Leaders are part of a hierarchy that oppresses, misdirects and hides their cowardice behind others' actions.

Instead, I will show you with my actions and outspokenness that one person as fucked up as you are, or maybe even more so, can do something, mean it, not back down and keep going. When I step into that courtroom on Feb 11th I am not only representing myself, I am representing all those who support me and my actions. I will be speaking to a courtroom of people. But also future generations of activists. Activists that will either feel empowered to save Animals' lives today and tomorrow, or activists that will be taught by example to fear the throng. If you think I would let down this movement or the Animals by folding like a lawn chair, then you truly do not understand the loyalty and selflessness of a wolf.

Animal Liberation, Whatever it May Take!

FAQ

This FAQ list is far from exhaustive. It could easily encompass not only a Part 1, but also Parts 2, 3, 4, 5. At some point, however, I will more than likely make it a full chapter which I intend to publish over the next couple of years. Please bear in mind that none of these questions are rhetorical in nature. I have, at one time or another, been asked these questions.

Please note the brevity yet substantive nature of my answers to these questions. In numerous conversations I've had with people about the relevant issues involved, the devil is truly in the details. Or perhaps better stated as the laziness, apathy and selfishness are in the details. This because as 'Screaming Wolf' says in the manifesto, 'Declaration of War,' "People derive their thoughts, and philosophies from what they already feel, not the other way around." And since many people perversely enjoy the taste of dead Animals more than they care for the truly autonomous nature of Animals. What they really desire is that Veganism and Animal Liberation issues be difficult to comprehend and therefore of little consequence.

So instead of acceding to this narrow mindset and wasting time in tediously long arguments I choose to provide statements and answers. In doing so I retain the moral high ground instead of acting as a supplicant begging for care and understanding. I put the ball firmly back in their court.

Another point of note is that some of these questions would only be asked by those already well versed in the issues of Animal Rights. This is directly related to the lack of material relating to the Abolitionist's philosophical and/or strategic stance within the Animal Rights community. In no way do I consider my answers/opinions the final say. Those who identify with 'Abolitionists' may find my answers either extreme or not extreme enough. All I can say is that these are my heartfelt opinions born of a deeply profound love of Animals, the seriousness of the issue and a great degree of activism; from leafleting, talking and in some instances taking the law into my own hands. If you find yourself in concord with any of my answers feel free to use them. If not, then carry on.

Animal Liberation, whatever it may take!

Questions and Answers:

-Why do you exclusively promote Veganism?

Many things are grayly subjective but within that gray area are points of black and white. Animal exploitation is one of those points of black and white. Just as racism is wrong under any circumstances so it is that discrimination on the basis of species is wrong. As such, you are making consumer based decisions that perpetuate Animal, slavery, suffering and death or you are not.

-Isn't being vegetarian a step in the right direction?

Certainly. However, it is not an end in and of itself. It's only good as a stepping stone to Veganism, and Veganism as a step towards Direct Activism.

-But most people drive cars and use public transportation. These modes of travel all use animal by-products in one way or another. That being the case is not absolute Veganism impossible?

Veganism, as most things in life is not about achieving perfection but about doing the best you can and consequently the least harm.

-What if you had to eat an Animal to survive?

If I found myself on a plane that crashed on the frozen tundra and I was the only survivor, and an Animal crossed my path, yes, I would eat it. Until that unlikely circumstance occurs, Go Vegan!

-But can't anyone help Animals, not just Vegans?

Of course. However, a child molester could also save a child from a burning house. That singular deed does not negate a voracious appetite for exploitation.

-So Being an Abolitionist Animal Liberation Activist is all about Veganism?

No. Going Vegan is only the first step. We Abolitionists not only oppose Animal exploitation in our own consumer decisions but also in the world around us.

-How do you do that?

In a myriad of ways. We protest, educate, liberate Animals from harm or death and we tirelessly endeavor to stop Animal exploitation by industry and those others who profit from this perversion. Whatever it may take.

-"Whatever it may take" seems to imply illegality?

Well, clandestine groups such as the Animal Liberation Front, Animal Rights Militias and Justice Department do work which is debatably illegal to stop Animal exploitation. They too are Abolitionists.

-So to be taken as an Abolitionist Animal Liberation Activist it is necessary to possibly break the law?

No. Most Abolitionists work well within the parameters of the law, but do not shy from supporting their comrades in the underground resistance.

-What are some of the other attributes of an Abolitionist?

No matter what tactics, be they above or below ground activism we struggle and/or speak out on behalf of and for the total liberation of Animals. We are not interested in changing the manner in which Animals are currently used and abused. We strive to eliminate entirely the use and abuse of Animals by people. Additionally, we do not place the base value of property over the true value of life. A business needing to turn a profit does not alter this dynamic. Sentient beings have an inherent right to live free and without human interference. We also have a sense of urgency that this exploitation be stopped in the here and now. Not endlessly lobbying for merely incremental changes to the status quo over conceivably decades.

-But according to Gary Francione, Abolitionists do not support illegal direct action.

Firstly, how would it have been possible to be an Abolitionist in the days of slavery and to not support the underground railroad. That would be patently ridiculous. It bears mentioning that not all Abolitionists were part of the underground railroad but certainly none were against it. In the second instance, Gary Francione is not an Abolitionist. He is a promoter of Veganism to be sure, but not an Abolitionist.

-Don't you think that some of the underground groups, such as the Animal Rights Militia, are going too far?

I do not think anything that has happened for the sake of Animal Liberation has gone too far. In fact nor could it. Anything that stops Animals from being murdered and/or stops their oppressors is of value. Anything that does not contribute to this goal is pointless.

-But isn't violence wrong under any circumstance?

The use of force insofar as the manner in which it is used varies greatly. A man raping a woman in a dark alley and a good Samaritan coming along and bashing in the rapist's head with a pipe is an example of violence employed for a greater good. That being, stopping the rape. Regrettably we do not live in a perfect world and sometimes force is required to stop violence. The reason certain individuals get squeamish about the use of force to save Animals is because, in their myopic worldview, Animals are somehow 'less than' and therefore not entitled to the use of any and all means to end their suffering.

-So you promote violence?

No. I promote Animal Liberation. In whatever form that may take to achieve this goal.

-What is Animal Rights 'Welfarism'?

The welfarist branch of the Animal Rights movement are composed of many of the larger groups. Such as, The Humane Society and many individuals such as vegan sellout Peter Singer. In the same manner as Abolitionists there are many factors that support the philosophical underpinnings of the Animal Rights movement. However, a totally unacceptable factor is an attitude of casual compromise with the exploiters.

-What characterizes a welfarist?

As organizations their main concern seems to revolve around money. They do this in attempt to expand their base of support. Additionally, they stick to the ephemeral and the more fashionable aspects of their version of Animal Rights. Examples include, puppies, kittens, free-range and cage free, etc. These being nothing more than empty platitudes, that certainly further their goal of raising money, but do nothing to truly advance the issue of Animal Rights in any substantive way. In many ways they are scam artists promoting something on the order of 'Animal Rights lite' to their adoring masses who think they are actually accomplishing something of value. They consist mainly of elitists who ferociously denounce the work of the true Animal Rights groups, the grassroots groups, if you will. In effect they argue that we should still use Animals but do it more nicely. Or in their words "more humanely." It beggars the imagination and defies credulity to say that it is possible to kill Animal "humanely." But their target audience eagerly laps up this pabulum. Using and exploiting Animals for any purpose is cruel and unusual. We can never be truly civilized until this societally sanctioned barbarity is stopped.

-As an Abolitionist are you opposed to pacifism?

No, not in and of itself. Different people have different propensities and obviously many of us are peaceful. We do, however, have a greater sensitivity to these issues to begin with. Regrettably, too often pacifism is a front for cowardice Martin Luther King, Jr. was a pacifist but never ceased to actively engage the system. He put himself and his followers in harm's way time and time again. He did not stop until he was assassinated. Direct Action is ninety-nine percent of the time non-violent, but it does require courage one hundred percent of the time.

-But what about arson as a tactic? That's violent.

I would disagree. Violence cannot be inflicted upon a piece of property it can only be destroyed. It's this attitude of "violence to property" that is the fly in the ointment. Violence can only be visited upon sentient life. Beings with an interest in being free of pain and suffering. If you punch a wall you've only done "violence" to your hand not the wall.

-But you eat plants, they are sentient.

No they are not. If they were you would take your carrot out for walk in the park and not your dog. If plants were sentient then there would be no difference between kicking a pile of leaves or a human child. Pointedly, if you really cared about plant life, you would go Vegan and quit supporting the voracious misuse of plant life and the natural world in general, some of whose most precious resources go to feed 'livestock' instead of people. Enough grain and feed goes into the production of five pounds of beef, an amount that would feed a Vegan for a month.

-If groups like the A.L.F. are doing the right thing then why do they wear masks and post their communiques anonymously?

Although the actions of groups like the A.L.F. are morally justifiable their actions are not recognized as being legal. Therefore they are required to act in all respects anonymously.

-If you were a business owner and someone destroyed your property how would you feel?

I would certainly not like it. But I am not an activist on behalf of business, I am an Animal Liberation Activist.

-Do you really believe that Animals feel pain as humans do?

Most certainly they do. They experience terror, fear, love, etc. The whole spectrum of emotions.

-How do you know?

Because I have empathy. If it is not plainly evident to you that an Animal is in pain it's either because you are in total denial and therefore lying to yourself or you are totally lacking in emotion and possessed of a perverse disregard for pain and suffering of any kind.

-Wouldn't you win more people to your cause if you were not so accusatory and extreme?

No matter your position or attitude on one thing or another there will always be those who agree with you or don't. The Animal Liberation movement is already rife with "lukewarm activists." Our purpose as Abolitionists is to effect change not to convince the morally blind. What happens to Animals is a form of the most horrific torture imaginable. In our opinion the response to such must be in-kind.

-Do you really believe the change you seek will come in your lifetime?

I do not know that answer to that question. I can, however, state unequivocally that nothing will ever happen as long as we, as a society, continue to accept the status quo.

-Don't people have the right to eat whatever they want?

No. They have the ability to eat what they want. True freedom means not doing whatever you want but doing what you ought. If our wants were allowed to run rampant then society itself would become unjust in the extreme.

-As a Vegan how do you get all your protein and nutrition?

I eat something that is Vegan, then wait about four to six hours, then I eat something Vegan again.

-Doesn't it take a lot of will power to be a Vegan?

Not if you truly care about Animals, as everyone claims they do. Also one must acknowledge the fact that it is immoral to use their dead bodies for your gustatory pleasure.

-So you don't think "free-range" is even a little better than "factory farms?"

No it is not. This concept of free-range this and free-range that still ultimately means the death of an Animal for our use. It is a total societal fiction that you can somehow 'humanely' allow an Animal to live and then kill it. (I addressed this in a previous question.)

-What about 'humane slaughter'?

This is oxymoronic. Perhaps you could explain to me how to 'humanely slaughter' (kill) an Animal.

-Why are you so concerned about Animals? There are a lot of people that need help as well.

I have no issue with helping people. However, Animals are exploited in vastly greater numbers than any group of people. From this stems my concern.

-Isn't Animal Rights extremism just another form of terrorism?

No. Militant animal rights activism is about saving innocent lives. True terrorism consists of targeting and killing innocent lives.

-Many vivisectors and fur farmers fear for their lives because of clandestine Animal Rights extremists. Isn't targeting them terrorism?

No. They take innocent lives and therefore are themselves terrorists. The A.L.F. is Homeland Security for critters. Those who torture, kill and exploit non-human Animals are not innocent bystanders, they are perpetrators whose actions must be stopped.

Final Statement to the Court in Colorado

February 11, 2011

I'm here today because I burnt down the Sheepskin Factory in Glendale, CO, a business that sells pelts, furs and other dead Animal skins. I know many people think I should feel remorse for what I've done. I guess this is the customary time where I'm suppose to grovel and beg for mercy. I assure you if that's how I felt I would. But, I am not sorry for anything I have done. Nor am I frightened by this court's authority. Because any system of law that values the rights of the oppressor over the down trodden is an unjust system. And though this court has real and actual power, I question its morality. I doubt the court is interested in the precautions that I took to not harm any person or by-stander and even less concerned with the miserable lives that sheep, cows and mink had to endure, unto death, so that a Colorado business could profit from their confinement, enslavement, and murder.

Obviously, the owners and employees of the sheepskin factory do not care either or they would not be involved in such a sinister and macabre blood trade. So I will not waste my breath where it will only fall on deaf ears. That's why I turned to illegal direct action to begin with, because you do not care. No matter how much we Animal Rights activists talk or reason with you, you do not care. Well, Mr. Livaditis (owner of the Sheepskin Factory), I don't care about you. There is no common ground between people like you and me. I want you to know that no matter what this court sentences me to today, you have won nothing! Prison is no great hardship to me. In a society that values money over life, I consider it an honor to be a prisoner of war, the war against inter-species slavery and objectification! I also want you to know that I will never willingly pay you one dollar, not one! I hope your business fails and you choke to death on every penny you profit from Animal murder! I hope you choke on it and burn in hell!

To my supporters, I wish to say thank you for standing

behind me and showing this court and these Animal exploiters that we support our own and that we as a movement are not going to apologize for having a sense of urgency. We are not going to put the interests of commerce over sentience! And we will never stop educating, agitating and confronting those responsible for the death of our Mother Earth and her Animal Nations. My Vegan sisters and brothers our lives are not our own. Selfishness is the way of gluttons, perverts and purveyors of injustice. It has been said all it takes for evil to conquer is for good people to do nothing. Conversely, all it takes to stop the enslavement, use, abuse and murder of other than human Animals is the resolve to fight on their behalf!

Do what you can, do what you must, be Vegan warriors and true Animal defenders and never compromise with their murderers and profiteers. The Animal Liberation Front is the answer. Seldom has there been such a personally powerful and internationally effective movement in human history. You cannot join the A.L.F. but you can become the A.L.F. And it was the proudest and most powerful thing I have ever done. When you leave this courtroom today don't be dismayed by my incarceration. All the ferocity and love in my heart still lives on. Every time someone liberates an Animal and smashes their cage, it lives on! Every time an activist refuses to bow down to laws that protect murder, it lives on! And it lives on every time the night sky lights up ablaze with the ruins of another Animal exploiters' business!

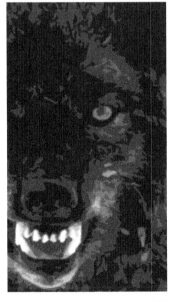

That's all Your Honor, I am ready to go to prison.

The Fight Goes On

I have been sentenced to five years in federal prison, the minimum sentence allowable in my case. At the time of this writing, it's the day after I received that sentence. My next stop is Salt Lake City to begin the legal process over again on my remaining arson and AETA charges. I haven't seen the media yet, but apparently they now have me pegged as a "pet killer." At this point, I have been vilified enough from all sides that it's losing its effect. I have been accused of petty thievery, homophobia, eating beef, and burning a meth dealer's pet (which is from the interview of my brother turned paid federal informant (and not a matter of any previous court record) in the house fire that I went to prison over in '97! And I am unaware of any such "pet" fatality.

In any event, if I was going to bring up the past to assassinate my character, I would go with the fact that I used to build slaughterhouses and not my vigilante justice against a drug dealer. At least in my mind, that's a much larger transgression since those machines I installed in 1995 are still killing Animals even as I write this.

Through these last seven months of jail, I have faced many personal challenges as well: The death of my beloved grandmother, Gwen; my brother, Trapper Zuehlke, seeking to utterly ruin my life for 35,000 bucks of reward money and some irrational jealousy of my successes in life (which, since our youth, he has harbored against me. I honestly don't know why); I've had reporters sweet talk me into interviews then show up and tell me that "there's a special place in hell for arsonists" and assorted provocative comments geared at getting me to froth at the mouth on camera -- All this while dealing with the stress of detention and court.

Anyone that thinks I enjoy any of the status that I have achieved in the radical Animal Liberation movement can forget it. I wear an orange jumpsuit and have spent 19 hours locked in a two-man cell every day since July 22, 2010. In my brief article, "Vegan Wolf Tribe," I thanked my supporters. At this time, I would like to thank my detractors and I do not mean that in a condescending way.

Anyone who has followed my writings should by now know that I say what I feel and I don't mince words. I thank my adversaries that have kicked me hardest when I've been at my lowest because you have taught me about myself. Many people in this world spend their entire life questioning what they are truly made of or even what the point of their existence is. I spent many times of my life feeling that way. I just accepted it as the fabric of everyday life or simply part of the human condition.

But if there is one thing I am sure of, it's that the struggle for Animal Liberation is fixed within my breast. No one can take that away from me! Not the media, not false friends or family, not the federal government and not the prison system. Last year I authored a communiqué that began: "The arson at the sheepskin factory was done in defense and retaliation for all the innocent animals that have died cruelly at the hands of human oppressors."

That is why I went A.L.F. That is why I am Vegan. That is why I write and speak out and it's the only reason. And this I now know because the system has continually spit it's invectives at me and not only attempts to demonize, but scare me, with their control over my physical body and their institutionalized authority. I must admit that without their oppression of me, I would have never known what I can withstand. But all this is over and easy to see and cope with.

What's been the most difficult for me is the pretentiousness and accusatory nature of members of our so-called liberation movements -- Animal, human or total. I used to think that if you fought the good fight with every ounce of courage and fierceness you have, you would be accepted and even loved by the "movement." But I have learned different.

The scrutiny, pretentiousness and exclusivity of many so-called Vegans, anarchists and radical environmentalists ensures that the ranks and numbers of these "movements" will never swell. It's hard enough to sacrifice your security, freedom and safety for others. But it's made twice as difficult when the message that gets conveyed to would-be warriors is that if you do not fit the political mold, you will be demonized by your "comrades" as badly as you would be by FOX News (sometimes worse). It is masses that revolt and change any form of oppression, not dinky groups of intellectuals and political science majors.

The evidence of this became apparent to me at sentencing yesterday. While I know that people stand in solidarity with me from all over Mother Earth and lots of people show their moral support online, after three months of rallying people to my sentencing, barely a dozen people showed up.

Nevertheless, it was the most successful day of my life for more than one reason.

First, I'm an emotional guy and seeing those that did show up and knowing the hard work that Elizabeth put in to organize on my behalf almost brought me to tears in the courtroom. I did not feel alone and I definitely felt the love.

Next, despite the US Attorney painting me to be a lunatic with a gas can, which I guess is his job, the judge did not have any personal animosity against me and even called me intelligent and commented that she enjoyed my writing. She said that she hopes I discontinue my career as an arsonist and become a full-time writer for my cause.

Next, I said exactly how I feel about the court, the sheepskin factory, my supporters and the direction of Animal Liberation. And, in so doing, I not only spoke out for the Animals, I won the personal battle of my life by not compromising my beliefs in the face of incredible adversity.

And, lastly, I want to say that I know there are a lot of people that look up to me and that is what these people need I suppose. But, in reality, I'm not Animal Rights Jesus and I'm not a lunatic with a gas can. I'll be the first to admit that I am, at this point, a serial arsonist. Again, it is what it is.

What I really am is a 34-year old man that comes

from a phenomenally-dysfunctional childhood and as such I am enraged by many forms of oppression because I've experienced many of them firsthand and under many extreme circumstances.

Despite the fact that I never made it past the eighth grade, I got my G.E.D. and put myself through trade school. I went Vegan because I care. And the only motivations for my actions and words are my love of Animals and my hatred of those that profit from their death. The only promise I can make is that this is my main concern. This is what I believe. I will be Vegan 'til my last dying breath because that's who I am...

Who the hell are you?!

In Defense of the Underground

There is a war. Every second 321 farmed Animals are slaughtered. Every year nearly 200 billion pounds of milk are produced by the rape of "dairy" cows. Nine billion chickens are murdered annually so that flesh eating bastards can dine on gore and filth. All too often we hear these numbers and they fly right over our heads.

Did you know that you don't even reach a billion seconds of age until nearly 35 years old? Are you aware that right now an Animal is being tortured to death by demons in lab coats, for entertainment, food, clothing, vivisection and any other trivial and redundant reason you can imagine? Animals suffer and die worse deaths than we can even wrap our minds around. And what do we do? We posture and pose. We debate the validity of tactics like arson because there may be a field mouse in the wall. How many bugs, snakes and nocturnal critters have you killed with your metal monster, I mean, car?

If you saw a man skin a cat in a field so that he could sell its "pelt" would you not run over and stop him because you might step on a mouse unseen in the grass? Give me a break. If these are your ridiculous reasons for not joining or supporting the Animal Liberation Front then you are a pretend friend to Animals. Let me guess, you're a pacifist. Yeah right, I doubt it. If you were in a cage being raped, beaten and violently tortured and murdered you would want someone to liberate you, stop your torturer with brute force and the building that they held you in to be burnt to the ground. You're only a pacifist when it's not your neck on the chopping block. I'd bet my life on it. What else, oh yes, you're a Vegan you're doing your part.

Non-participation in evil is obviously the first step but our Veganism is not saving any lives. The human population is growing, on the day you or I went Vegan 100,000 kids got weaned into flesh as food. And Veganism doesn't turn you into an instant activist, only being active can do that. Example, I am not a rapist, I never have been, I never will be. But wouldn't it be dishonest for me to represent myself as a rape prevention activist? Simply because I don't engage in said behavior. Well if it's that easy to be proactive then I'm also a human rights activist, I'm an activist against child molestation, I'm an activist against domestic violence. Actually there are so many evils I don't participate in, I am actually solving the entire world's problems, by not doing anything!

Hmmm... how conveniently lazy and apathetic. Actually if you find a behavior or system of abuse deplorable the least you can do is not participate in it. Then you have the militant posers. You've got every Earth Crisis and Hardline Vegan album and t-shirt ever made. You look the part and talked the talk better than the rest. In fact the more years you pose like this the more others in the scene respect you. Once in a blue moon you go to a protest so that you can knock the dust off your balaclava and get some pictures of yourself looking like an Animal Rights ninja. And if I called you out on your bullshit to your face you would say something like, "you have no idea what I do when the sun goes down." Yes I do, you go to bed. The only time you should put a bandana on your face is if you are cleaning a chicken barn at a sanctuary or about to kick ass for the Animals. To do otherwise is to disgrace the institution of radicalism and makes a mockery of the sacrifices of real Earth and Animal Liberation warriors.

There are many ways you can help Animals and the movement for their total liberation. The most powerful way is to become a direct activist. That means centering your activities and tactics around endeavors that either directly help and save Animals or directly confront their exploiters. Something you can do to help Animals are work at a sanctuary or help them out with a few bucks since caring for Animals can be costly. Or you can do a home demo, you can let an Animal exploiter and their neighbors know that killing Animals or profiting from their dead bodies is sick and wrong and will not be tolerated. Or best of all you can join the underground resistance and make the most impact.

Since 1976 the Animal Liberation Front has been saving Animals' lives and shutting down places of abuse and harm. The ALF has also educated the public through hundreds of communiqués that not only is there cruelty going on behind the scenes but that it will not be tolerated. Actions for Animals happen nightly all over the world. But there are others in the underground as well. The brave and noble warriors of the Animal Rights Militia and Justice Department employ all the same tactics of the Animal Liberation Front but are not restricted by a philosophy of nonviolence. I think that's great. Anything that stops Animal exploitation is of value and anything that allows Animal use and abuse to continue is unacceptable.

Even as I write this I can hear the hysterics of apathetic Animal Rights activists misplaced contention. Really, why don't you lose your marbles over the fact that US soldiers have been murdering brown people in the desert for over a decade straight? Where's your outrage when police execute blacks on camera and in public? True to pacifists' hypocrisy you aren't appalled by violence, you're appalled by unsanctioned violence. This is because many of our own activists are as insane as the society they live in. If you are more freaked out by the statement "not restricted by a philosophy of nonviolence" than you were the statement "every second 321 farm animals are slaughtered," then this is testimony to your faulty morality. The issues of Animal abuse and death are incredibly serious for the individual beings involved. To them it is unimaginable wickedness. Morally, it's depravity at its worst. Because not only is it unnecessary killing, it's the murder of innocent beings which compounds the evil. The environmental impacts are staggering as well. Deforestation and grazing for livestock go hand-in-hand. Fifty-five percent of all drinking water is used for the raising of that "livestock." Waste runoff is the number one polluter of the other 45% of that drinking water. Any way you look at it, you cannot build a just system off the most cruel objectifications in the world's history!

We treat Animals with no regard because they are the least able to defend themselves in an organized way. And from there, all the way up, the hierarchy of exploitation you get used and abused according to your inability to defend yourself from attack. What a sad and sick construct. There is such a thing as cause and effect. Spiritualists call it karma. No matter what you call it, it's unavoidable and inescapable. In the case of Animal Liberation, what it means is you are not going to fight and succeed against the most proactive evil that our animal sisters and brothers endure by eating soy yogurt or lighting candles. Industries that make billions of dollars off systematic murder don't stop because of morality. If they had a shred of decency they wouldn't have gotten into that business to begin with. They stopped because they are fought and they lose. It's the only language that any bully understands.

Now I don't expect every Vegan to spring into action and become a warrior for Animals… obviously that's not going to happen. But badmouthing and standing against those that are actually saving Animals or taking the fight for their freedom to the exploiters' front doors and businesses is unacceptable. I will tell you here and now that you disgust me and you have no idea the risks that we in the underground take. And all that we sacrifice to be who we are. Until you couch surfers and armchair generals can match your high and mighty opinions with actions then those opinions are invalid. This is a war and the Earth and Animals have hardly any human resistance on their side. As long as Vegans and so-called Animal Rights activists succumb to compassionate apathy, then the rest of us are obligated to become firebreathing fanatics. You can't escape cause and effect.

When I was arrested I had in my backpack a copy of a manifesto entitled, "Declaration of War," by Screaming Wolf. It is the single most dynamic and powerful manuscript for Animal Liberation I have ever read. While parts of it are dated, its principles and programs of action are timeless. Read it, reread it, let its truths empower you and then become a liberator. If that is not within your realm of possibility, then start an Animal Liberation Front support group. Help an actual Animal, protest aggressively, if you're not Vegan, go Vegan. Do something besides hiding your cowardice by attacking other's bravery!

Right now in Mexico the ALF and ELF are leading the way in activism and have been for years. They are shining example for us all to follow. Support them and our imprisoned comrade Adrian Magdaleno Gonzales, who is Vegan in a Third World prison and remains defiant in the face in of adversity. Until society stops exploiting Animals, we are at war with society. Until there is an end to the destruction of the planet, there will be no end to the destruction of property. As long as they are is an enslaved Animal and an exploiter for pleasure or profit, then there will always be someone to take the place of an imprisoned ALF activist.

Animal liberation, whatever it may take!

Vegan Resistance

Many of us that take a militant or hard stance on the issue of Animal Liberation have been approached at one time or another and asked by other so-called activists why we don't spend more time people-pleasing and politicking. The general idea is that if you appeal to people's conscience instead of their outrage, you will win more people over to "the cause." Perhaps you can attract more flies with sugar than vinegar. However, like most welfarist ideology, there is a lot of oversimplification and faulty logic to contend with.

First off, large numbers of apathetic people are not a victory for Animals. I would rather have ten Vegan warriors by my side than 100 or 1000 keyboard commandos that won't so much as show up to a demo and hold a sign. More importantly, ten Vegan warriors can make a huge difference for Animals now.

I get mail from activists from all over the country. I see the successes from the accounts and media that they send me. And the success stories are always the same. They protest passionately, they put the pressure on the abusers be they puppy mills or vivisectors, they refuse to be intimidated by the authorities and, because of their passion and actual resistance, the media begins to pick up the story. The businesses shut down or have to move their operations.

This is moral. This is the correct path of action.

The idea that tactics are right or wrong is an elitist and cowardly approach. It is only the ends that are right or wrong. If yelling and protesting angrily work, then they are moral because the end goal is to be effective against animal abuse. But, if your end goal is for everyone to think you are a nice person, then yelling and aggressive protest are clearly wrong. And this is the line between those that truly care, the above ground, and those that are simply posturing, albeit compassionately.

Another untruth is that "by being aggressive you will turn others off to the cause." The truth is, like attracts like. If you promote Animal Liberation with militancy and fanaticism, then that is the type of person you will attract. And that is what this so-called above ground movement needs. Lukewarm activists are turning veganism into a diet fad and animal rights into a philosophy. Well diets and interesting conversations are not saving Animals. On the contrary, they condemn Animals to die by the billions while those that claim to be their protectors play games with words and remain "passive fellow travelers."

It's time for this movement to be effective instead of affected. I am unimpressed with how much you identify with the Animals' pain and suffering or how you're "crying all the time for the Animals." I'm unimpressed for two extremely important reasons.

First, how you feel doesn't matter to an Animal doomed to death. You could feel happy and excited that they are going to die or sad to the point of a nervous breakdown. Either way, your feelings have zero effect on an Animal in a cage.

Second, I doubt the sincerity of such statements when they are made by those not actively engaged in the fight against animal exploitation. If you care, then you act! If you hear of or witness Animal abuse and your reaction is to weep and wail and then continue to bury your head in the sand, you are overly affected.

My advice to you would be to continue to view the gore and exploitation until you work through your ultra sensitivity and begin to get angry about it.

As I have said before, the proper response to evil is outrage! The reason that it's a proper response is because outrage fuels physical resistance whereas fear, sentimentality, and tolerance do not. In our above ground -- and by "above ground," I mean ferociously legal Animal Liberation movement -- the individual must take the initiative. The individual must be motivated! Because, ultimately, it's pro-activity that makes you an activist.

Surfing the internet and commenting on Animal Rights websites is not activism. Thinking about the issues and formulating opinions is not activism. True activism resembles work because that's what pro-activity is. Time, energy, and self-sacrifice add up to results.

If your idea of Animal Rights is hobbylike in nature, then please find another hobby. If your idea of activism is being Vegan and nothing more, do not call yourself an activist. While I'm very glad to hear whenever anyone goes Vegan, simply not participating in an evil is not the same as actively opposing it.

Any form of evil or oppression is incredibly active and working hard at subjugating. Non-participation does not stop it any more than war stops because you don't join the army. And this IS a war -- a war with more casualties than any other before it! How many billions of gallons of blood must spill before we act? How many more atrocities have to occur to the most defenseless of us before there is a sense of urgency in the here and now? Apparently for most, no amount of suffering can call them to action, no amount of the suffering of others that is.

What is this compassionate apathy? This caring laziness? It makes about as much sense as "humane slaughter." I call out this welfarist, hippie-crit nonsense for what it is because it is turning a resistance movement into a consumer product and image, an empty shell. I also defend militancy and direct activism strongly because, for decades, we have been under attack by groups and individuals too numerous to list here. As we press forward, speaking truth, saving Animals, and bringing the fight to the doorsteps, office buildings, and pocketbooks of Animal exploiters and profiteers, we not only face scrutiny from the media, but also cling-ons and do-nothings of our own "movement" that seek to hide their own inaction by tearing down another's hard work and sacrifices. **It ends NOW!**

There is only one movement -- the one that moves! You want to partake in it? Then get active, get passionate and confront, agitate and educate. Study other social justice movements before us that have had levels of success that we have yet to reach. Groups such as the Black Panthers, John Africa's MOVE!, American Indian Movement, and Suffragettes all employed winning tactics -- tactics that work when employed by any group, no matter what the cause. The words of Malcolm X, Screaming Wolf, and Sitting Bull are timeless and just waiting for us to rediscover and apply them to today's liberation struggles.

It's time to not only embrace "security culture," but also reject "paranoia culture." The Animal Liberation Movement has so much in common with so many other struggles past and present. I want to see us united in a struggle for the total liberation of earth, animals and humans. But before we will ever be taken seriously by others, we must take ourselves seriously. Real recognizes real. And, until we quit begging for care and understanding like supplicants, we will never attain the warrior element that it takes to not only win battles and save our animal sisters and brothers, but also attain a truly revolutionary status which we must because a change as radical as freeing the enslaved only happens by force of will. Those who profit from slavery and death only stop when they are made to. And so, it is time for us to draw that line amongst our own -- a line between those of us that would see this filth and gore end now, by any means necessary, and those that want to look good and do nothing. You're either part of the solution or part of the problem.

Animal Liberation, Whatever It May Take!

Our First Responsibility

On more than one occasion, activists or Vegans have asked me what they can do to be more effective against Animal exploitation. In this article, I am going to discuss our first responsibility to our Animal relations. No matter who we are or where we may find ourselves, this responsibility never leaves us. That responsibility is to speak for those who cannot speak for themselves. I know it sounds simple and elementary and usually when I say that to one of my Vegan sisters or brothers I get that look like I am being semantic or too basic with my advisement. But it is not such a simple task and it's vastly important that we as individuals and groups of individuals master this elusive skill.

Anytime we speak third party, it's difficult to not throw in our own opinions, beliefs and emphasis, actually it's nearly impossible. But in the broader sense, an overabundance of personal projection will invariably lead to a completely compromised message. So then the questions arise: how do we speak for others not even of our own species? What statements can we make that apply to all species of sentient beings? What are the most effective and important points to make on behalf of our Animal family?

Let's look at these questions one at a time:

1. How do we speak for others not of our own species?
First off, we speak out in their favor. But in order to do that we need to be speaking from the heart and not just our heads. There is nothing wrong with intellectual and reasoned arguments but they can be taken to a fault. As anyone seasoned in the art of debate knows, if you are lever enough, you can find logic to nearly any side of an issue. So before we speak up and speak out we must understand that our voice is for them. We must understand that we are going to purposefully fashion points of our conversation in favor of Animal Liberation

94

because that is how we feel. We love Animals. We love the Earth. When we fashion our intellectualism around our love, passion and ferocity, two incredibly important things happen. First, we will attract other passionate people. Second, no matter what the outcome of the conversation, you will speak authoritatively instead of playing on people's sympathy which always comes across as weak.

Next, when we speak for the Animals we do not need to be constantly concerned with how people will take it or if they can handle it. This overly concerned mentality of how your points will be perceived leads to all kinds of problems and compromises. Our responsibility is to say what needs to be said. Not how people will take it. Trust me on this... I know I can write a brief paragraph and 100 people will see it from 50 different perspectives. If you become worried about how everyone takes things, you will quickly find yourself constantly explaining what you meant. No matter what anyone thinks about a statement like, "Animals exist for their own intents and purposes, not human ends," it is incredibly important that it's said.

There is a very faulty logic that welfarists and supplicants embrace. It's an idea that every little subtle point made may one day blossom into that person turning into an uber-conscience Vegan. More in keeping with reality is that you're asking too much of people. You cannot expect people to connect the dots on their own just because you did. This kind of compromised approach leads to the single issue syndrome. Anti-fur activists that drink milk, prairie dog activists that go out for burgers after a demo and so on and so forth. But statements like the aforementioned or, "Your rights end where another begins," better explain why it's never OK to use another for their body or by-products. Whether they are a cow being, sheep being, bee being or human being. Which brings us to the next question.

2. What statements can we make that apply to all species of sentient beings?

This question is a large reason why I prefer the term "Animal Liberation" instead of "Animal Rights." The term "Animal" is used as a blanket statement – it covers so many critters and various forms of life that it's hardly adequate when it comes to considering autonomy and individuality. That said it's still a very applicable word primarily because our kind is in a constant state of oppressing all kinds. With our food choices, technologies, societies, and constant attitudes of human supremacy. And this is truly the difference between "human" and "Animal." Ours is a premeditated subjugation. Indeed you will never find an elephant that enslaves bees so they can dine on their puke. But since species vary so radically in so many ways, their individual rights in accord with human use become profuse. And just the cataloging of each being's "rights" is an exercise in futility. But since human use and abuse is their common problem, then liberation from that use and abuse is the answer. At the end of the day, Animals do not need our love, and people constantly exploit the objects of their "love."

Animals need us to leave them alone. We need to love Animals because as humans we will never fight and sacrifice for others in any meaningful way unless we feel a strong or powerful emotional connection like love, hate, or true empathy. So in answer to the question, what statements apply to all sentient beings? It is those which speak to their total freedom from human usage. This is more than mere Abolitionist rhetoric. It's an honest assessment of the wishes and desires of others. If you give a hen the choice between death by factory farm, a life of laying eggs in a "free range" prison or a coop on a family farm, she will choose freedom from any human use every time. So as long as the Animals are Abolitionists, we should be too!

3. What are the most effective and important points to make on behalf of our Animal family?

First and foremost, we need to always challenge the validity of Animal enterprises. The idea that meat eaters need Animal flesh, the idea that hunters need to help control Animal populations, the idea that Animals want to be used by humans, or the idea that God has given us dominion are pure bullshit! People profit off of, or are in some way personally gratified by, Animal exploitation and murder. All their arguments to the contrary are just word games to justify what they want to do in the first place. Another important point that can always be made is that speciesism is involved in all of our decisions to use Animals. Practice reciting a person's answer back to them, only replacing the Animal with a human to expose what they are truly defending. You can do this very effectively in nearly any conversation or debate.

Examples include but are not limited to:

Vivisection
Statement: "It is OK to experiment on Animals because they aren't as smart as humans."
Answer: "So why don't we experiment on the mentally challenged… they're not as 'smart' either."

Animals for food
Statement: "People have been eating Animals for thousands of years; it's natural."
Answer: "Men have also been raping women for thousands of years, incest has been taking place for thousands of years. Even more to the point, cannibalism has been around on a global scale up until about 3,500 years ago. So are these abuses also 'natural' just because they've been around for a long time?"

Animals for entertainment
Statement: "They are fed and taken care of, they have it better than they did in the wild."
Answer: "So if we sentenced you to a life in a cage and put you on display, you would be doing better than the people in the free world because your meals are free?"

The ways in which you can use this tactic to expose speciesism are the limitless and very effective. As far as debates are concerned, like I said in the beginning of this article, it's vastly more important that we speak the truth for Animals and their agenda of Animal Liberation than we often think. A compromised voice for others invariably leads to compromised actions. And the next thing you know, you're back to the Vegan tupperware party seriously thinking that brownie and cookie recipes are activism.

Giving voice to those that have none is a primary function of a Vegan ethic. Veganism and animal liberation are not just a diet or a way of thinking. They are an ethic. One that is quickly becoming lost and co-opted by producers of products and consumer driven markets. Honestly, I don't have a problem with the dietary promotion of Veganism. Because if the masses are ever to embrace it, then it must be marketed to them at some point. But in a rush to win converts over to this lifestyle, the message and higher conscience that accompany it have been dumped by the wayside. This is why nearly all my writings have been and will be targeting my own Vegan and Animal Lib communities. Because until, and unless, we start straightening out our own thinking on the relevant issues, ethics and bottom-lines, we will forever lack cohesion, radicalism and the teamwork necessary to move these mountains of murder. And personally, I find it rewarding to be able to shake my Vegan sisters and brothers out of their doldrums and replace it with a zeal and passion.

Even if I can only reach you a few at a time, because I am much like you, I never feel like I am   doing enough for Animals. It seems the more active we become the more that frustration can grow. It's simply a symptom of being a caring person in a cruel world that you cannot immediately change. I too have stood in awe at the horror and callousness that our kind inflicts on all kinds, have had nightmares and terrible feelings of guilt and shame for all those I cannot save because I am just one, little imperfect person raging against institutionalized cruelty. And I have eaten a piece of Vegan cheesecake with glee because, just like many of us, my inner child is a fat kid with his hand in the cookie jar. But I have also come to understand that nothing great is won for ourselves or others without great sacrifice, hard work and focus. And I would rather die fighting these injustices than go along with business as usual for even one more day. And if that's how you feel inside, then we truly know each other even though we have never met.

Animal Liberation, whatever it may take!

Supreme Vegan Power

Consumerism truly has affected our ethics and the ways in which we behave. Even many that think themselves progressive, liberal or fire-breathing anarchists. We are taught by advertisers to think in terms of profitability instead of principle. For instance, when it comes to Veganism many people I have met like to debate its validity of effectiveness as a tactic. And no doubt I understand the validity of many of those critiques. As I have written more than once, "For every one of us that go vegan, 100,000 kids get weaned into flesh as food." That being said, Veganism is still an important first step and moral imperative. From a theoretical standpoint, if everyone did adhere to Veganism all these disgusting and evil animal enterprises wouldn't even exist. This is what Bertrand Russell calls a "universal truth" in his book, "Why I am not a Christian." He says, "If you can take a behavior and extend it infinitely [in a social context] and it is still good for all, then that behavior is a universal truth." From a fundamental standpoint, it is morally wrong to use the dead bodies and by-products of the slavery of any being that has an interest in freedom or desire to live free of pain and suffering. The circumstances under which you use them do not matter.

Using Animals' dead bodies or secretions is morally outrageous whether off a store shelf or out of a dumpster. Would you eat the dead and broken bodies of child laborers left in the trash? If not, why not? They're just going to waste otherwise. Besides, you didn't purchase them thereby perpetuating their exploitation. You would not eat them because it's wrong to participate in their use under any pretext short of starvation. Just as slavery and racism are wrong to engage in whether or not your participation is perpetuating the problem. Or whether your non-participation is stopping the problem. Speciesism takes many passive forms and first world "freeganism" is one of them. We are Vegan because the problem is not in how we use animals. The problem is that we use Animals. Once you open the door of interspecies objectification, it is a Pandora's Box from there on out.

So why is it wrong to use others for food, entertainment, clothing, vivisection, etc.? What is the reasoning behind our "let live" ideology? It is this: "Your rights end where another's begins." Contrary to consumer driven society, every time you have a craving or desire it does not mean you have a right to fulfill that craving. Just because you have five bucks in your pocket does not mean that you deserve things. Animals have a right to live their lives free from human tyranny. Just like you do. Anything that crosses that line is not a right. It is an ability and should not be tolerated or protected as if it was somehow valid. This is why an Animal's right to live or be defended by any means necessary supersedes any businesses' ability to profit from their exploitation, or death. "Your rights end where another's begins" is also why it is never alright to make the conscious decision to choose Animal products. Of course, the only loophole to that is starvation or if you literally have no other option for survival. But at that point you're not making a consumer decision, you are choosing to live instead of perish. A completely different plight than dumpster diving at Pizza Hut or eating a slaughtered being at Thanksgiving because you are choosing human tradition over the life of an innocent bystander of human avarice.

Animals' right to be left alone by humans supersedes human foibles and traditions. Nor should we fall for slick little mentalisms like comparing "-ists" or "-isms." Many times when I have promoted or defended veganism as a natural and superior lifestyle I get microcosmic arguments thrown in my face like "the indigenous" rebuttal. The short version of this argument goes something like this:
You say - "People need to go Vegan!"
They answer - "What about indigenous people? Why should they have to succumb to this Western idea? Why should they have to change their already decimated culture even more to suit this white man's ideal?"

This is the oversimplified version, there is much more

to the indigenous argument. And I agree with it 100 percent! Unfortunately, most often the person making the argument isn't as concerned with protecting the rights of tribal people as much as they are trying to equate Veganism with racism. And as I said, it is a microcosmic argument. Last time I checked, white people were not traveling to the rainforest or Arctic and forcing Tofurkey and Almond Breeze on the Natives. Furthermore, I am completely alright with hunter/gatherer societies living how they do, in accord with their surrounds and even yes, eating Animals. But I still think the other 5 billion people on the planet should go Vegan!

Also, I do not subscribe to the idea that it is alright to kill Animals with impunity because you are brown or have cultural reasons for doing so. Sorry but I am an Animal Liberationist activist and there are several thousand species, varieties, and types of Animals globally suffering terrible lives and deaths and even extinction at the hands of speciesist, humans oppressors in America, Mexico, Canada, China, India, Australia, Europe, Africa, and elsewhere.

We are not racists or sexists. We are not imperialists or bigots. We are Animal Liberation activists. We are Abolitionists and as such we extend our compassion, concern, ferocity and energy towards the liberation of all life. If that interferes with anyone's human supremacy, so be it. The idea that you must choose humans or Animals isn't always the case, but if we must, then we choose Animals. Why?

Because they are innocent. Deers do not dress up in urban camouflage and come to your neighborhood and shoot you in the face and then mount you and your family's heads in their living space. Chickens do not build mechanized slaughterhouses and raise genetically modified and domesticated people to murder at a break neck pace, or enslave us for eggs. Animals do not make up ridiculous religions that demand human sacrifices to appease the imaginary men in the sky. They do not "farm" us for our skin, eat our brains, make twisted sex video involving our deaths, involve us in cage fights, put our children in veal crates and force feed them liquid diets. They do not beat us up in rodeos, stab us to death in crowded arenas, mount our skulls on the front of trucks! Elephants do not enslave or beat us until we perform for them like puppets, tigers to not sentence us to a life in a cage so that they can display us in a zoo, snakes do not skin us alive to make us belts, etc. etc. etc!

No. These are human pursuits, through and through, am I wrong? There is a good reason to make designation between humans and Animals and it's not because humans are superior. It is because our depravity, perversion, and lust for blood as a species is profound and disturbing! It's true that there are many factions of mainstream Veganism in America and Europe that are ruining the purity of the Vegan ethic with their classist, soccer mom, yuppie bullshit! But I think it would be a profound mistake on the part of a militant Animal Liberationist to just let elitists like Francione, Peter Singer or any of their ilk completely ruin our way of life without a fight, because a lot of us are not them. I have met Vegan Rastas (from Jamaica). I have known and helped with a Vegan soup kitchen run by blacks and for blacks in the inner city of Denver. I have read hundreds of communiques by Vegan Warriors of the ALF and ELF of Mexico. I have met Africans that have killed poachers in Africa. And I myself am Latino. Many Food Not Bombs groups feed the homeless Vegan meals every week. Most of the Vegan and AR community are predominately women. So this idea that Veganism is a white or elitist culture is an image that advertisers perpetuate so that they can hike up the prices by putting big green V's all over packages.

But if we won't hold onto Veganism and its ideals then it continue to get stripped of its vitality and truth. Until one day being Vegan will be as silly as being on the Atkins diet. Since I went Vegan, I have seen us go from being viewed as "those crazy Animal Rights people" to "those trendy hipsters and white yuppies." I'd rather be the Animal Rights looney myself, not a supplicant begging for approval and validation from right wing assholes or thin-skinned lefties. This world is meant for all beings. Get it! Got it! Good!

Animal Liberation, whatever it may take!

Resist to Exist

I am an anarchist.

I'm not the politically-correct hipster anarchist.

I am not the rhetorical anarchist either.

Reading dry accounts of the various factions of anarchism has never held much interest for me. I am an insurgent, an opposer. Why? Because I was born that way. When I was in kindergarten, my teacher, Ms. Whirly had a parent/teacher conference with my mom. I remember her saying something about me being a very bright young man but that I had serious problems with authority and one day it would get me in a lot of trouble. I do, and it did.

I came to find out that school doesn't want you to be a 'bright young man.' Serious questioning is the enemy of primary and secondary schools' indoctrination of youth. While my grade school teachers prattled on and all the kids answered in unison, I sat at the back of the class reading about dinosaurs, mythology, and astronomy. It made me feel hopeful that places or times existed that were far from here... far from Iowa's Aryan education... times and places where humans weren't the center of the entire universe. Luckily my parents were far from conventional. My father was a half English, half Bohemian musician and my mom was a hot-tempered Puerto Rican that believed in the mystic powers of Earth, Animals, and Nature. My father's father died in World War II fighting the Nazis and he always has a serious contempt for government as a result. He was also devotedly atheist and very anti-racist.

One thing I always loved about both my parents is they never cared to conform to the uppity idiocy of their immediate surroundings and they also allowed me to formulate my own opinions. No one in our house went to church. I didn't have to get involved in little league or cub scouts or any of that. The only rule in our house was you learn to play an instrument. I chose drums. When I was 7 years old I learned "Cocaine" by

Eric Clapton and the 50s hit "Johnny Be Good." Music proved to be the love of my life. Music and resistance.

By age 10, my parents divorced and I was in Denver Colorado with my mom. We lived in a duplex with my aunt, her boyfriend, my Gramma and Grampa, 3 cousins, and a steady parade of family friends. Talk about culture shock! In any case I became close with my cousin Eric. He was 5 years older than me and lived in the basement. Eric did whatever he wanted and was largely ignored. He was the kid downstairs. Every time a teenager came over with spiked hair or tattoos it was a quick hello and then down to the basement. Of course my aunt and mom didn't want me to hang out down there. "Let the older kids be left alone," they would tell me, but it was to no avail. The first time there was no adult supervision in the house, downstairs I went. It was the most amazing place my young eyes had ever beheld! On the old beat up record player was a band by the name of Dead Kennedys. It sounded like the Beach Boys on Ritalin! There was crazy banners and posters everywhere. Pentagrams, circle As, cryptic lettering. I was in love.

My cousin introduced me to his friends, all teenagers. But even though I was just a boy they didn't mind me at all. On that day I figured out that I was an anarchist. Within a couple years I was playing drums with my cousin and his friends and was officially part of the Denver hardcore/metal/punk underground. I'm happy to say that the core group of kids that was to me like family never seriously changed, 20 years later we are still all irrevocably anarchist. Of course outside of that solid 5 of us everyone else came and went. But for us it was not a phase, we found bedrock.

By the 8th grade I refused to go to school. Although I still love to read and learn it's a decision I never regretted. School for me felt like 8 hours a day of getting my soul murdered with boredom and chalkboards. I would much rather be skateboarding on private property or breaking things. But that was then and this is now. The only thing that's really changed for me was the sureness that only comes with life experience. Now in my mid-thirties I realize more than ever how much people and their governments suck. Systems of control everywhere you turn. Get married, have kids, buy a house, work for some evil corporation 'til you die, buy a car, buy a bigger car, watch t.v., get drunk, don't think, just consume. No thanks, I'd rather eat a shotgun. I'd rather have a girlfriend than a wife. I don't have any kids cause most of 'em I meet act like loud mouth little drunk people.

I didn't buy a house cause it seems like a hassle and impossibility that the bank will ever let me own it. I have worked for some stupid places but in exchange for exploiting me for labor I stole everything I possibly could. So I broke even on that one. I didn't learn to drive 'til I was 25 and even then it was very infrequent. What can I say, I'd rather ride. I threw my t.v. in the trash years ago because I don't like plastic rectangles or squares with technicolor trying to indoctrinate me with the hive mentality of a 10 Watt human existence. I don't drink because alcohol turns people into slobbering, vomiting idiots! Honestly I don't know, it just comes natural to me. I think back to the doldrums of the classroom or the evil of the slaughterhouses I've worked in and I'm reminded that things are not okay. I see Christian scumbags peddle their sanctimonious trite to the peoples of the world as if it were 'the good news' and I'm reminded that many people have shit for brains. I see the country of my birth wave its' red, white, and blue murder rag as if it stood for more than anything short of genocide and used cars!

Then I look at the shackles on my own feet. The cuffs and black box digging into my wrists and the dinky confinements I'm kept in and I am reminded that cops, feds, jailers, judges, deputies, correctional officers and all their ilk are the agents of repression, the haters of true freedom, the enemies of social justice! The betrayers of the Earth, Animals and all life!

How can I remain defiant?
How can you remain complacent?!

I guess that's just what's in your nature. It's a shame though, really it is. I won't pretend I understand or even empathize, cause that would be a lie. I'm a wild animal myself and domestic breeds are largely a waste of my time. It's a fact that this domesticated world hates the wild and free and it's also true that many sheep like to run around in wolves' clothing writing their little books admonishing people about the evils of civilization. Trying to motivate others to dismantle what they're too cowardly to themselves.

Everyone likes to talk big, write big, and pose like they're for real.

So few are, so don't believe the hype.

And don't believe anyone that can't back up their talk. You'll know a wolf by their teeth, not their howl. And I'm proud of that. All the traps and trials I face are worth it. All the persecutions and oppressions of my person, I won't run from them. If I could go back to April 30th, 2010 and reconsider the arson that I'm now sitting in prison for, I wouldn't change a thing.

Life is meant to be free. Not murdered, skinned and tanned then sold and perpetuated for profit. Life is meant to be defended, not subjugated.

This sick and twisted human supremacist culture does not dictate what's right and wrong. Not for me, not ever. Western civilization has rivers of blood on its hands, I don't. A good Christian-American patriot is partaking in one of the worst cultures and traditions of genocide in the history of the world! The only real crime of groups like the Black Panthers, American Indian Movement, and Animal Liberation Front are challenging state sanctioned authority or having the courage to fight fire with fire. The only faith I have is that it won't last forever. Oppression and power-madness sooner or later will implode.

Contrary to the capitalist or industrialized worldview, we live on a finite planet. We can only bleed the Earth so far before even our technology will not allow billions of people to breed endless minions of ever-fatter, ever lazier, and ever-degenerated generations. My faith is that one day the Earth will flood and burn the human parasite off it's back and if I have the great good fortune to witness even the beginning of that process, I will gleefully go down with the ship, laughing all the way. And honestly why should it be otherwise? You get out of things what you put in. So it should come as no surprise that when you build huge mechanized "civilizations" off of the blood and bones of suffering and murdered Animals and the decimation of the natural world, that at the end of the day you will reap what you sow. How hard is it to comprehend that a fair and equitable society will never come from the rape, murder, and theft of its indigenous population, or the slavery and displacement of a race. As surely as $2 + 2 = 4$, oppression + murder = self-destruction, whether by violent revolution or moral degradation.

Do I seem negative in my world view?
Do I come off as apocalyptic?
Perhaps. But I think I'm just being a realist. I fight for a moral, peaceful, and just world. That's been what I've sacrificed much of my time, energy, and now my freedom for. But I do so because I'm optimistic. If humanity were on trial, the overwhelming evidence in the case would point to cruelty, subjugation, and greed. And on the other side would be a handful of actual freedom fighters whose caring and courageous stands throughout history get immediately co-opted by sign holders, petition signers and a bunch of feel good faddists.

Only now am I starting to truly see the writing on the wall, only now am I realizing how intuitive me and my friends were as little punk rock kids. The angst and passion we had is what makes real changes. The only reason it ever even fades is because we let it. So many people write off extremism as inherently flawed, but is it? A very real case could be made for extremism in the cause of liberation. It's those that don't compromise that the rest hold their comparisons up to. And it's the militant that keep things on target when the others get distracted and forget their movements, their causes. How shortsighted the compromises are, how forgetful of the acute wrongs are the welfarists and fair-weather activists. And in their lukewarm ideology they create forgetful movements of paper pushers and people pleasers. But it's not an endless cycle that can rise and wane. It is a finite world as I said. And sooner or later we will reach the end of the line.

Greed and apathy will become played out to their inevitable end.

So now I sit in my prison cell and read about dinosaurs, mythology, and astronomy and I remain hopeful that not only have there been times and places free from menacing human hands but that, one way or the bloody other, there will be again.

Total liberation, whatever it may take!

Green Is the New Rage

Please do not consider me a "Green Scare" defendant and please do not become scared to be "Green." Better yet, please do not be scared to be militant, or outspoken, or an activist for the legal aboveground or clandestine underground. Still better, don't give in to state-sanctioned fear.

Once you do, you're being reactive and that's what they're counting on. Also, you are giving the security forces of Animal exploitation too much power... power they don't deserve!

Instead of concerning ourselves with how big and scary the FBI is or how ruthlessly they target activists, we should be concerned with flexing our own muscle and shutting down Animal use and abuse wherever it occurs.

At times, I fear that the bulk of the Animal Liberation "movement" has really and truly forgotten that this is a selfless cause. Our aim is to stop Animal objectification, whatever it may take.

And as a movement, we need to be empowering each other to act... not scaring the shit out of activists under any pretext. It's a fact that the ALF, ELF, and aggressive legal activists are in the crosshairs of the power structure — not just here, but globally. The only way that will change is by becoming ineffective welfarists that never rock the boat and are literally in cahoots with abusers or by not compromising the Animals lives and keeping ourselves and our movement on the frontlines and in the trenches, kicking ass and taking names.

Or, I suppose you can also become one of the paranoia crowd and just throw the agent provocateur label at anyone that refuses to submit to fear. I hate repeating myself, but I guess I must. This is a War! I do not say that for the sake of drama or literary emphasis. One major flaw with many people within Animal Lib is the stuck-on-theoretical mindset. We see these abuses to Animals in vivisection, meat, dairy,

112

and eggs, or fur and then we start filing it away as, "what this means in a social context and what tactics have the most universal appeal to other humans" when we should be asking ourselves practical questions like, "how can I start fighting these abusers?" Or, "where can I have the most impact against these cruelties?"

How can I save an Animal today or stop these atrocities now? Even for just a few critters. Because that's the context we so often miss. It's about Animal autonomy, not about how the government turns on the people that care about the Animals. But while I'm on the subject, it's nothing new!

Those in power abuse that power to smash resistance to the status quo. It's as old as the hills. Every single movement for progressive change has faced a system that has turned on them with vengeance and often violence. Look at the Black Panther Party for Self-Defense. A mere 43 years ago, there were 150 Panthers, political prisoners, locked up in the prison system.

Various police and feds were executing these brothers and sisters because they were demanding an end to institutionalized racism that was destroying their communities and they were not going to back down, no matter what!

Also, amongst their own people, they were at times blamed for their hard stance bringing down the heat and making it hard on everyone else. Predictable. Within our own movement, it's nothing new. Antivivisectionists were actually called "terrorists" over 100 years ago! Ronnie Lee, the founder of the Animal Liberation Front, was being called a "terrorist" in a court of law in 1982.

In the larger context, these persecutions, whether of the individual or the entire movement, are only a landmark on the road to success, the only time they are in vain is if we stop fighting!

And I will tell you this, we are only beginning the Abolitionist movement for total Animal Liberation. How many more trials and tribulations will we endure before we will set the captives free? So don't be shocked or deterred because of what they do to me or any other political prisoner/ POW. Of course, support us in our times of tribulation, but don't make our sacrifices be in vain. Don't let this system use us to scare you! Speaking for myself, I knew what I was in for when I became an ALF operative.

Part of being an outlaw is accepting the consequences, or at least making peace with them before you ever act. A complete change in attitude is needed.

When our activists speak out and tell it how it is, the only repression they should face is from the enemies of our Mother Earth and our Animal Nations, and then, that should be seen as the breach of our right to free speech. That it is. You have the right to say what is happening, you have a right to say what the solutions are, you have a right to your own opinions and you have a right to fight against murder, torture, and slavery.

You have those rights because you assert them, not because a government agency tells you that you do! So what's the proper response to "the Green Scare?" How about "the Green Rage?" Yes, that's it!

Consider me a Prisoner Of War and a proponent of the Green Rage! It's not 9/11 anymore and this is not FOXNews - so no militant Earth rights activist or self-respecting anarchist should be defending or limiting their actions in accordance with government witch hunts. If you look at the communiques from the underground in the last 18 months, thousands of Animals have been saved from death. The ALF was active in 32 countries and only 7 underground activists were caught (including myself) worldwide! In the above ground in America, vivisectors and their associates are feeling the heat. From down South all the way to the West coast! It's time to bring back the good ol' days where solidarity was an action instead of a salutation… and ideas did not take the place of activism.

It's okay, the internet will still be there at the end of the day.,, after you've put your back into your beliefs. I promise! And I'm sure millions of otherwise grown adults will still be arguing and gossiping on it like little angry children. They might even tear you down because you weren't around for ten hours to defend yourself. And who knows? After effecting real change, taking a real stand, or getting your face licked by an actual Animal that's alive because of what you did, you may not even care what the armchair generals and theoretical wizards were commenting on today.

Animal Liberation, Whatever it May Take!

Always Looking Forward

Since my arrest I have been asked a couple of questions frequently by supporters. The two most asked questions are, "What was it like being in the Animal Liberation Front / Underground?" and, "What's it like to be in jail or prison?" In this article I will answer both of these questions to the best of my ability.

But first, I must admit certain experiences in life are initiatory and as such cannot truly be conveyed accurately through the medium of words. This has its good and bad points. For me, as an individual, I am very grateful that this is the case, for it has shown me that certain things are sacred and secret. I am reminded that sometimes word jugglery is simply inadequate no matter how elegantly stated.

When I think of the Animal Liberation Front, the first thing I feel is a feeling, not a thought. It's a feeling of true solidarity with every other A.L.F. warrior. The fact that I do not know any of them does not weaken it -- it strengthens it. The fact that we come from different countries, speak different languages and may hold different beliefs on a myriad of other issues doesn't weaken it -- it strengthens it! Because all that is truly and deeply important in this sisterhood and brotherhood is our actions and Animal Liberation, no matter what the obstacles. We are the woe of all Animal abusers everywhere. And we are self-liberated, more than most. When I think of my tour of duty in the A.L.F., I recall the most triumphant, free and intensely tumultuous times of my life. So with that said, here are my answers to...

"What was it like being in the Animal Liberation Front / Underground?"

Being an A.L.F. warrior can be a life of duality, extremes and often opposites. Before I went underground,

116

I worked as a manager of dry goods in a health food store. I never attended any seminars or workshops on how to become an Animal Rights ninja or pyrotechnic professional. This is reality, not an action movie where you need to have some dramatic climax of events and a bunch of training. All that is needed to begin an underground campaign is the desire to act more than talk or posture. Unfortunately many Animal Lib activists never so much as make this crucial step. We seem content to play the pacifist victim role: "I'm crying all the time for the Animals," and, "I wish I had the courage to do what needs to be done" are common themes amongst the so-called compassionate.

My transformation from a legal activist to a clandestine one came on the day I finally decided that I couldn't stand one more hollow conversation about 'The Big Picture of Our Movement' or anymore rhetoric about how cruel this or that person or practice is. At that point I decided to quit my job. (I'm not suggesting that's necessary... it was just my path to the underground.) I had no vehicle so I knew that anything I did would be local. I also knew that sooner or later someone would want to talk with me about the actions I had in mind. Therefore, I thought it would be best to not be so accessible as to be in one place, day in and out, forty hours a week.

The first reality check I had was about practicality. Being homeless for me was no easy task. I honestly was not good at it. I had passed the age where hipster anarchists would want me as a part of their neatly manicured communes and squats. For all the talk about diversity in such circles, most collectives I encountered were small cliques of 20-somethings that had nearly identical backgrounds and worldviews. I, as a 30-something Vegan Straight Edger wasn't exactly a natural fit.

So, during my time in the A.L.F., I couch surfed when I could, and slept in parks when I had to. I stole my food when I had no money. (I've always felt that quality vegan food tastes better stolen.) I began to settle into a life of drifting. I found that after the arson of the Sheepskin Factory in Denver, I no longer had the urge to talk about Animal Lib issues incessantly and to no great effect. Nor did I need anyone's approval or denial. This is how I knew I was on the right track.

While living homeless was a new tribulation in my life, the empowerment of direct actions more than made up for it. My worldview shifted from the philosophical and theoretical to the tactical and actual. And here entered the beginning of extremes in my life. By night I was picking targets and burning 'em down. But by day I played the part of goofy overgrown Straight Edge kid just out for a bit of travel.

I made my way to Salt Lake City, Utah. My reasoning for doing so was that Utah has been one of the most targeted states in America for A.L.F. activity and also has a large and often extreme Straight Edge community. If there was anywhere that I could blend in and not stick out (as much as you don't stick out with half your face tattooed) it would be there.

Once in Utah I had a couple decisions to make. First was if I was going to continue my campaign. Looking into the recent history of Animal and Earth Liberations I know that once the FBI was on the hunt they would use their resources for years to discover or frame someone. I also knew that sooner or later when they began questioning or infiltrating activist circles in the Denver area my name was bound to be at the top of the hardcore Vegan list. My next thought following was that once they discovered I suddenly left town, I would be more of a person of interest. So the reality struck me that I had crossed the Rubicon and in examining my thoughts and feelings about that, I decided that it was time to proceed further.

The next decision to ponder was organizational affiliation. I had not yet claimed the arson at The Sheepskin Factory in any communiqué. I had in my possession the manifesto "Declaration of War" authored by Screaming Wolf. I felt then as I do now that it is the best book ever written as pertains to the reality of Animal Liberation and the tactics that must be employed. And my own personal philosophy on radicalism and militancy is definitely more in keeping with clandestine groups like the Animal Rights Militia and Justice Department.

However, I became an underground illegal direct activist in part because I was sick of posturing. And the truth is I would never seek to do personal and actual violence to anybody, unless it was in defense of myself. So if I'm not gonna go to that level, why portray or posture as if I would? Also the reality thus far is that with all the great actions of underground affiliates such as the A.R.M. and J.D., and contrary to their threatening and 'violent' communiqués, many of their actions are of a certain shock value.

Don't get me wrong... I understand that evil unpunished and un-avenged will be continued without end. And I am in no way a pacifist. Sometimes it takes force to stop violence -- that is the reality of the world in which we live. But at the end of the day the Animal Liberation Front is the only group that's been as continuously active globally, has rescued several thousand Animals under cover of darkness and caused several millions of dollars' worth of retribution to Animal users and abusers everywhere. That's why I chose to become an A.L.F. operative.

My next two targets were the Tandy Leather Factory in Salt Lake City and the Tiburon Restaurant in Sandy, Utah. I choose Tandy Leather for many of the reasons I torched The Sheepskin Factory in Denver. They are a business that profits from Animals being skinned, often alive, for no other reason than to take up hobbycraft with their dead bodies.

Tandy also sells the dead skin of many other once vibrant and living creatures, such as ostriches, snakes, lambs, etc. When I broke into Tandy Leather, I lit the bolts of leather and cash register on fire to show my distain for the practice of profiting from the blatant murder of not just the Animal Nations, but also Mother Earth, which is daily poisoned with cancerous and hazardous chemicals from the tanneries that supply Tandy Leather stores nationwide.

This sick capitalist system wants to always concentrate

on these perpetrators, as if they were victims. I don't buy that, not for one minute. Because if they are the victims of injustice, it is only the same 'injustice' that the slaveholders suffered when robbed of their slaves. It's only the same form of 'injustice' that the Nazis suffered for just going along with orders and being 'good Germans'. And it's the same 'injustice' that Christians perceive is out to get them even though they run the entire western hemisphere of the globe!

The victims are the piles of dead and broken bodies that wanted to not be skinned alive for a buck… not their task and slave masters.

Next I went after Tiburon Fine Dining. This was a restaurant that sold the notoriously cruel product foie gras, which for the uninitiated is bloated goose or duck liver that is obtained by forcing an 18-inch feeding tube down the victim's throat. The other end of that tube has a trigger on it that shoots the food into the stomach, much like a garden hose would water. Of course no Animal wants to be force fed to death, so they are kept in cages that confine all movement, so there is no chance of escape.

I lit Tiburon on fire on July 2nd of 2010, but I had meant to do it two days earlier. However, when I showed up there were a few cars in the parking lot and I could not be certain that there was no one inside, so I left.

By this point the stress of my lifestyle was beginning to catch up with me. I went to bed that night wondering if I should just call it quits for a while and put my own life back together. That night I had a very vivid dream that protested against that notion.

I dreamt that I had gone to the Tiburon Restaurant just to see the inside of the place and when I went in I saw a dining room packed with well-to-do rich people eating other people! They were gluttonous and relishing their cannibalistic urge for flesh. In my dream I was scared and sickened almost to the point of nausea. I awoke that morning partially amazed that these issues weighed so heavily on my subconscious and also struck with the realization that if it were people that were the victims of Tiburon, I would not so readily abandon my campaign.

So I found my reserve and went back to finish what I had started.

After the arson at Tiburon, the stress of the lifestyle was wearing me down. I knew I needed a break.

I had recently contacted my brother through Facebook and had talked to him a couple times via a payphone. (My phone was off -- apparently you have to pay the bill every month.) My brother was concerned about why I was roaming around the country homeless. For once the roles were reversed. Even though my brother is exactly one year and two days older than me, I have always been the one to have my shit together. That said it felt good to be the one in need. And my brother, now married and with kids, seemed to have some assistance to offer.

It must also be said that my brother had a very drug addicted, violent and criminal past. With these things in mind, I made a fatal flaw. I told my brother, my flesh and blood, what I had been doing. My exact words were, "Google 'The Sheepskin Factory'... That's what I've been up to." The first website that came up on his search was an Animal Rights website. From there he looked up accounts of the arson from the mainstream media and found out there was a cash reward for any info leading to the arrest of the person or persons involved.

48 hours after that phone conversation, my brother was a federal informant. Over the next 3 weeks, the FBI taped my phone conversations (my brother had wired me money to get my phone turned back on) and followed me around Salt Lake City. My brother wanted me to go back to Iowa, the state of my birth and the same state he still lived in. I can only guess that this was where the feds had originally intended to take me down. My brother once again wired me money for

a bus ticket to Iowa. I decided to go back to Denver so that I could keep a couple bucks. My intuition was telling me that something was not right, but I had surmised that after setting fire to two Animal exploitation businesses in just under a month that it was paramount that I leave Utah quickly. It never occurred to me that I was running into a trap.

Looking back, it should have been obvious, but hindsight is 20/20. In any event, when I arrived back in Denver, I contacted my brother and told him of my change in travel plans. He told me that our half-brother, who I know of, but have met only once, was living in Denver (which I knew was true), and that he would be coming out to help him move. He told me we could meet up, then catch up on old times, and of course he would have a few bucks for me.

For two weeks I lived in a park in downtown Denver while searching for temporary employment. At this point let me say that the authorities have done their job well – and I'm not talking of their arrest of me. What became evident to me living in the underground is that there is no actual support for the A.L.F. When I first began my campaign, I approached a well-to-do 'militant Vegan activist' in Denver and alluded to the fact that I was now underground as evidenced by the news on The Sheepskin Factory arson. This was a person that liked to brag about how much money she had to support all the "real and hardcore Animal Liberationists in the struggle." But when it came down to it, I was not only denied a single penny, but I was also no longer welcome. The "Animal Rights community" is so scared to be green that they've become yellow!

In the 80s and 90s, there were networks of aboveground support and actions in North America took place much more frequently. Now to be in the A.L.F. is to be a leper and to be found out by other "activists" is to be shunned and forgotten. Welcome to "militant animal liberation" in current day America. A whole lot of tasty food, conventions, big talks, large books and cowardly bullshit!

But I digress… back to the story. So I met my brother

at the Ramada Inn in downtown Denver. The first thing on my mind was that it was nice to be in the hotel instead of the park. My brother was calm and cool, no hint of anxiety. We began catching up on old times and he began speaking to me candidly about past criminal activity that he had been part of. With my defenses down, weary from the road and the street, tired and hungry, I made another fatal flaw.

I gave my brother a detailed account of my campaign. He asked me if I was gonna stop to which I responded, "No, not until they catch me or kill me." I told him of my plans to leave the country and then come back at a later date to resume my campaign. Everything was being taped by the FBI.

After we talked I asked my brother to drive me to the northern suburbs so that I could talk to a former employer about some work. On the way to Northglenn, we talked about family affairs and such. I was happy to be with my brother I hadn't seen in over a decade, I was happy that I would be sleeping in a hotel that evening and I thought everything was starting to look up. My brother dropped me off and gave me a hug and a kiss. As I happily exited the car my last words were, "See you tonight bro… love ya!" He drove off and I went to talk to my former employer about construction work.

There didn't seem to be anything immediate but there would be some drywall work coming up in a couple weeks. I headed off on foot towards the bus stop. Northglenn was the suburb of Denver I had spent my teenage years. My grandmother used to own a house just a few blocks from my former employer and two houses over from him was a house that my aunt lived in for many years as well. She had since moved and sold her home to the Robbs, a family that also had roots in Northglenn. As I walked by my aunt's old house, the Robbs were having a barbeque of dead Animals. They said hello and I walked up into the front lawn to talk for a few moments. And then, as fast as lightening, the ATF, FBI and Joint Terrorism Task Force descended upon me, guns drawn and ready to shoot… I was under arrest.

"What's it like to be in jail or prison?"

The ATF drove me to Glendale to be booked in. That is in South Denver. Before we arrived at the police station, the ATF took a detour by the burned out remains of The Sheepskin Factory. The thing about being arrested for arson is that everybody assumes you are a compulsive pyromaniac. I'm sure the vehicle I was being transported in had cameras in the cab. Unfortunately, the sight of a burned building doesn't make me laugh hysterically or even start rubbing my hands in excitement.

Once at the police station I was put in a small interrogation room with two detectives and an FBI agent. I was told, and I quote, "You will now be given the opportunity and privilege to talk to the FBI." My response was, "I have nothing to say." The agent then threatened to arrest my brother (which he knew was their number one snitch) simply for having talked to me. I said nothing. Then he had some dialog with the detective in front of me about how, "it looks like he doesn't want to help himself." I stared at the wall behind their heads and remained silent. And that was it: five minutes of not talking. And no other agent has ever questioned me again.

Next came what I like to call the system and the media fucking with me. First I went through booking in Glendale for 3 hours. Then I was transported to Denver City Jail and sent through booking for 13 hours. Then I was allowed to sleep 2 hours before my initial court appearance and moved again to Golden, Colorado for 8 more hours of, you guessed it, booking.

For nearly two days I barely ate (nothing is Vegan except fruit in the sack lunches you get when you're in Receiving). I got 2 hours of sleep and kept getting passed from one deputy to another at various County Jails, and aside from fingerprinting me and processing me in, they kept up with the questions which I refused to even acknowledge, let alone answer. Then finally, a cell and sleep.

The next morning I was awakened by an inmate pounding on my cell door, telling me, "Come out here (the commons area outside our cell), you're on The News!" I stumbled out into the pod and watched myself on T.V. All I remembered from that new story was that mugshot was the worst picture of me on earth! The next media I saw about my case they said I was arrested at a BBQ eating beef burgers! I was pissed off that the media had sought to make me look like a hypocrite and joke, with their lies. Looking back now I can see that I've grown. I no longer care what the media says about me, or anything for that matter. But upon arrest, it was a big deal to me.

As far as what my time was like in jail in Golden, Colorado, it was difficult. County Jail is the worst part of doing time. Since most people that come to county are going to leave within 30 days, it's not set up with much to do. In Jefferson County I was locked down 19 hours a day in a two man cell the size of a small bathroom. Most of my cellies were detoxing heroin addicts or petty criminals.

Another part of County time that sucks is all anybody wants to talk about is their charges or their case, which, when you're facing serious time, you spend a lot of your day wishing you could focus on anything else.

Here is another truth about doing time. Whether you are in County Jail, prison or the hole, there are things about that facility you will like or dislike (in comparison to other jails that you get carted around to). For instance, although I was confined to my cell a lot in Jeffco (Jefferson County), they fed me a Vegan diet! My meal trays came to me with a computer printed sticker that said "BOND, VEGAN" in big letters! And I also had an amazing view of the mountains.

As far as dealing with the inmate population, that was not difficult either. First off, whether inmates agree with you or not, they tend to respect a person that stands up for their beliefs. Secondly, jail and prison work by a kind of pecking order. Part of that pecking order is related to the severity of your crime. The only true outcasts in prison are sex offenders and snitches. So as the new guy when I'm asked, "What are you in for?" and I respond, "3 federal arson charges with domestic terrorism enhancements," it immediately puts me in the class of serious criminals. Third, I'm outgoing and good with people. Jail is full of people, so it's a trait that serves me well. And lastly, I am admittedly somewhat of an alpha male with an abrupt temper (it's not my fault… I'm an Aries).

I guess the best advice I could give anyone that finds themselves in prison or jail someday is this. Walk with pride, be respectful and don't be eager to buddy up with people; let them approach you. And most importantly don't make a big deal about it. Yes, it sucks. Yes, I would rather be anywhere else. But millions of people are in prison and they cope and survive. It's all just a part of fighting this evil empire. Or being poor, or black, or native, or "illegal" or a pothead, or… you get the idea.

There are however additional stresses to being a prisoner of war or political prisoner. The first letter I ever received in Jeffco was from some anonymous person accusing me of being a hypocrite and joke to all "real Animal Rights activists". As the weeks went on I began getting printouts from the internet about all the movement chatter. People seemed upset that I had too many tattoos and rumors abounded.

The first interview I granted was with some 50ish academic establishment animal rights welfarist creep. He showed up to the jail, started poking fun at my tattoos and began his interview by saying, "I'm wearing a leather belt. If you could, would you choke me with it?" I said, "Only if I thought I could get away with it." He actually scooted his chair back a little. Next he told me that his mother's house had been burned down by an arsonist and that he strongly disagreed with my tactics to which I responded, "Then don't employ arson as a tactic." Once we got into the issues of Animal Liberation, I debated him with savvy until he admitted that I really did know what I was taking about.

I left that interview with a bad taste in my mouth. Instead of allowing the system's media and divisive elements within the A.R. community to pick me apart, I decided to fight back with my pencil. The first article I wrote was entitled "Why I Am Vegan". In it I detailed my path to Veganism and Animal Liberation. Having built two slaughterhouses as a teenager, I saw firsthand the grotesque evil that happens to animals in food production. I'm happy to say that internet article was posted far and wide and well received.

The support mail began rolling in. If there is one thing that I look forward to every weekday in jail, it's mail call. I cannot stress enough how important it is to write prisoners. When I am fatigued or overwhelmed, it's supportive mail from like-minded people that keeps me going. It also reminds me that I'm still someone to somebody out there. Prison is geared towards stripping down your sense of worth. As time rolls by, it's easy to give up on everything and just become part of the prison politics.

So I began to write more articles and my supporters, etc. Not only has writing been an effective way to stay active in Animal Lib, but it's been a great coping mechanism. The courts always try to scare you into not speaking out along with their lawyers. The idea is for you to just sit there quietly, let the media vilify you, let the system use you to scare any other would-be militants and of course grovel and beg for mercy as if you were in front of God Almighty.

What a crock of shit! Many people have asked me how I am able to remain defiant through all this and that's a simple answer. I care more about the Animals and my beliefs than I do about myself. All the big talk you hear about how much we Vegans care about the Animals no matter what the price, well I actually feel that way. Plus I guess I just don't feel like kissing anyone's ass, be they business owners or the U.S. government. I'd rather go down swinging than degrading myself. But that's just me, that's how I roll.

That said, I wrote my final statement to the court in Colorado about two months before sentencing. It took me about 45 minutes. I sat down at the desk in my cell and just let it rip. My thought process was, "What would I say if I had no fear and nothing to lose?" Writing it and speaking it in court were two different things. On my day of sentencing I was a nervous wreck. Saying my final statement felt like looking down the barrel of a gun and saying, go ahead shoot me! To my surprise I received the mandatory minimum sentence of 5 years.

Great news to be sure, but unfortunately there's another shoe yet to drop, and that shoe is called Utah. Early on in the court process I tried to have my Utah charges dealt with all at once while in Denver. Being as all my charges are federal and not state, meaning that my crimes are not legally seen as crimes against Colorado and Utah, but against America, I can be tried for any of them in any federal court in America. The word that my attorney and I received from Utah was a definite no. I was to be tried in Utah separately.

After sentencing in Denver I began my three weeks in transit to Salt Lake City. Denver and SLC are a nine hour drive from each other. But before I was to go west, I was flown east to the Transfer Center at Oklahoma City. Upon arrival I was separated immediately from the other forty or so inmates. I was told I would be held in the special housing unit or SHU, which is just a way of saying the hole. In the SHU you have a shower in your cell and you are locked down 23 hours a day. When I asked why I was not going into general population, a corrections officer came over with a clipboard and said, "You are part of the Animal Liberation Front. That is a security threat group to the United States of America. While you're here, that's where you'll be."

For five days I was in a cell in the SHU by myself. But for my last two days I had a cellie, a small Hindu political prisoner from Singapore. He had basically been kidnapped by the CIA and brought to America because he gave a friend a ride to the airport and that friend was under investigation for gun running to Al-Qaeda. My feelings were mixed. While I was happy to not be alone in my cell and my cellie was an educated and interesting man, it really began to strike home that they (the FBI) seriously think I'm a terrorist.

A couple days later I was in the air again, but instead of landing in Salt Lake I was taken to Nevada Southern Federal Detention Center. During the booking in process it looked as if I would be going to general population and then the gang coordinator took me to the side to ask me some "routine questions". His first question was, "So are you some kind of terrorist?" I said no. His second question was, "Are you some kind of activist?" I said, "I am affiliated with the Animal Liberation Front." And so I was taken to "administrative segregation" – another fancy way of saying "the hole". I was kept there for ten days this time with no cellie. But I did have an interesting neighbor that was a high ranking member of the Mexican mafia. On our hour of recreation outside in the kennels (narrow fenced in cages for U.S. convicts in the hole to pace in for an hour a day) we would exercise vigorously together.

As far as my Vegan diet was concerned, both federal facilities worked with me on it. Hole time is more boring than anything. But once again, there is an upside. In prison you are hardly ever alone, so I took advantage of the solitude and did some meditation and stretching practices and a lot of exercising. Then back on the plane once more and on my way to Salt Lake City.

At his point, I had been doing county time for 8 months and after going through an entire court case in Colorado and transit to Utah, I was getting very tired of county jail and court proceedings. Upon arrival at Davis County Jail in Farmington, Utah (which is where I am currently awaiting sentencing as of the time of this writing), I requested a Vegan diet, which is usually my first priority entering a new facility. I was told I was not even allowed a vegetarian tray for spiritual reasons (which is standard at any jail or prison I've been in). I had to fast for my first two days, until my lawyer could get a court order to make the jail feed me vegetarian meals (I am still Vegan, but I must pay out of pocket for Vegan commissary items to supplement what I can't eat on my vegetarian trays.)

As expected, Utah has been a different experience

than Colorado. As far as the jail itself, it's not bad. I have more freedom of movement than in Denver and I am able to receive books from the publisher, so I've been reading a lot. I also have more time outside, which is nice. But that's where anything positive ends.

As concerns my court cases in Utah, the U.S. Attorney's office wants to turn my current 5-year sentence into a 15 year sentence and perhaps more. Apparently, it's a big deal that I gave a heartfelt and provocative statement in Colorado. Since my extradition to Utah, I have been made aware on more than one occasion that my beliefs and words are far, far more damning than my arsons. Instead of the system being focused on my "crimes" which did about 60,000 dollars-worth of damage, as compared with the 500,000 dollars-worth of damage done in Colorado, the focus is on scaring me into shutting my mouth at what may be my only opportunity to open it.

Given that everything is "terrorism" these days, I am under no illusions that the prison system is going to house me in some fluffy Club Fed. So I speak out not only as one that defends, fights and cares for our Earth Mother and her Animal Nations, but also as a man whose pride will not allow himself to be bullied by the powers that be. The decisions I make and words I speak are for the future, with the hopes of an upsurge in activity, activity that truly liberates Animals and permanently stops their exploiters.

Usually this is the point in my article where I write my inspiring and radical high note to leave the reader feeling empowered. But in this article I will end on a note of distress. My apologies in advance.

I am not your hero, or your mascot. As long as that's what you're looking for, that's all you will ever find, and I promise you that you will always get let down. Every time you find a Keith Mann, Barry Horne, Rod Coronado, Peter Young or Walter Bond, all you have found is a person that decided to take matters into their own hands. And we cannot teach you how to do that, because that's your decision, alone. At times I am embarrassed by what I see. Animals suffer and die and we do nothing. The real heroes of Animals are those who work at sanctuaries or otherwise directly impact an Animal's life for the better. The only "militant Animal Liberation community" is the A.L.F. and the underground. Of course there are many things that must be done and doing something is always better than doing nothing. But why settle so small?

A gangster will protect his evil enterprises with violence and his own life is ready to be sacrificed at any moment. But we self-proclaimed betters won't even risk social alienation. Cowards, fakes, frauds! If you care than prove it! Not to me, but to yourself! No matter where I end up or what happens to me, my cell, for however long I'm in it, will have a mirror, and I will always be able to look in that mirror and know there's a real motherfucker looking back at me! And there is no potluck, convention, conversation, website, flyer or workshop that will ever compare to that!

So this is my last, unsolicited internet article that I will be writing for a while. Of course I am always open to interviews and will always respond to support mail. My next stop is sentencing on October 13th of 2011 in Salt Lake City, Utah. After that I will make the transition from county jail to federal prison where I will begin writing a detailed and definitive book about the Vegan Hardline, a syncretic philosophy, program of action and way of life that can and must succeed.

Until the next time remember... don't sing it, bring it! And don't talk about it, be about it! As for me I will continue always looking forward.

Animal Liberation, whatever it may take!

Final Statement to the Court in Utah

October 13, 2011

I'm here today because of the arsons I committed at The Tandy Leather Factory in Salt Lake City, and the Tiburon Restaurant in Sandy, Utah which sells the incredibly cruel product foie gras. The US Attorney wants to give me the maximum sentence and beyond, not because of my 'crimes,' but because I am unrepentant and outspoken. My intuition tells me that this court is not going to show me mercy because I became 'suddenly sorry.' So instead of lying to the court in a feeble attempt to save myself, as I'm certain many do when they face their sentencing day, allow me to tell you what I am sorry for.

I am sorry that when I was 19 years old I built two slaughterhouses that are still killing Animals, even now as I speak. I am sorry that Tandy Leather sells skin that has been ripped from the dead, and often live bodies of such Animals as cows, ostriches, rabbits, snakes and pigs. I am sorry that the leather tanneries that supply Tandy Factory, poison the earth with dangerous chemicals. I am sorry that the restaurant Tiburon profits from the force feeding of geese and ducks until their livers explode, so that rich people can then use that as a paté for crackers and bread. I am sorry that they make a living from the dead bodies of wild and exotic Animals. I am sorry that we live in a day and age where you can rape a child or beat a woman unconscious and receive less prison time than an Animal Rights activist that attacked property instead of people. I am sorry that my brother was so desperate to get out of debt that he flew from Iowa to Colorado just to get me in a taped and monitored conversation for reward money. I am sorry that I am biologically related to such a worthless little snitch! I am sorry that I waited so long to become an Animal Liberation Front operative. For all of these things, I will always have some regret. But as far as the arsons at the Leather Factory and Tiburon go, I have no remorse.

I realize that the laws of the land favor a business' ability to make a profit over an Animal's right to life. It also used to favor a white business owner's ability to profit from a black person's slavery. It also used to favor a husband's ability to viciously attack his wife and act on her as if she were an object. Those who broke the law and damaged property to stand against these oppressions were also called 'terrorists' and 'fanatics' in their time. But that did not change the fact that society progressed and is still progressing along those lines. So today I'm the bad guy. That is just a matter of historical coincidence. Who knows... perhaps a less brutal and less violent society will one day exist that will understand that life and earth are more important than products of death and cruelty. And if not, then to hell with it all anyway! Whether my supporters or detractors think I'm a freedom fighter or a lunatic with a gas can makes no difference to me. I have spent years verifiably promoting, supporting and fighting for Animal Liberation. I have seen the Animal victims of human injustice -- thousands of them -- with my own eyes and what I saw was blood, guts and gore. I made a promise to those Animals, and to myself, to fight for them in any way I could. I regret none of it, and I never will! You can take my freedom, but you can't have my submission.

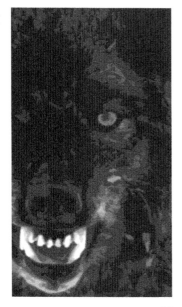

The Importance of Straightedge

Part of having a revolutionary mentality means we examine our beliefs and actions and then discard those which don't fit in the world in which we want to live. We first make this change in ourselves and then initiate that change in the world around us.

I want to live in a world where the Earth and Animals get to live and flourish. I want to live in a world without racism. I want to live in a world where our mothers and sisters are not preyed upon in the streets or in their homes. I want to live in a world that has respect for all innocent life, and I want to live in a world without the self-destruction and diminished capacity of inebriation.

To that end I am Straightedge. This means that I have taken a lifelong oath to abstain from recreational drug use. It further means that I have vowed to try to make this world a more peaceful and just place by standing against oppression, slavery and death, whether self-inflicted or otherwise. It is this stand that makes me Straightedge and not merely drug-free. It is a difficult oath to live up to and should not be undertaken by those that are not 100% sure that they can live up to it.

If I had to make a criticism about the modern day Straightedge movement it would be very similar to my critiques about the Animal Rights movement. Too much talk and thought, but not enough walk. This is much more true of Straightedge than the various liberation movements, mainly because for decades Straightedge has been a youth movement that revolves around music. I think that's great. I wouldn't ever deny a kid the fun I have had as a youth in this very same music scene. But the reason that so very many kids break edge in their early to mid-twenties is because sooner or later the show is over. And getting together to dance and sing-a-long about how much you love your friends runs its course.

This is why I've always felt that the radicalization of Straightedge as a liberation struggle of its own is important.

Because it gives kids a new focus and challenge with Straightedge beyond dance moves and hoodies. Thus we enter Vegan Straightedge. In North America I'm proud to say that the A.L.F. and Vegan Edge have always had a very symbiotic relationship. Throughout the 90s, Hardline bands like Vegan Reich, Raid and Green Rage got the youth focused like a laser beam on radical and fanatical Animal Liberation activism by blending the best elements of the struggles for Earth, Animals, anti-racism and anti-capitalism with the seriousness and purity ethic of the fundamentalist. All to a soundtrack that became more metal and less punk. It worked! With the power of discipline and a program of action.

It took more than one underground support zine to cover the nearly constant A.L.F. actions that took place for 8 years straight! That's because the music was not an end in itself, as it has now become. It was a successful and deliberate recruitment effort, a very successful one which, no matter what our personal speculations, saved hundreds of thousands of mink and shut down several Animal abusers forever.

I do not think that Vegan Edge has sold out or become weak compared to those days. I think there is just a lack of direction. A kind of drift that has taken place in the last decade. I feel that a partial reason for this began back in the 90s. It's fairly obvious that the oppression that Animals endure follows the same patterns, relationships and psychology as many human forms of oppression, i.e. racism, consumerism, capitalism, etc. There is no denying those correlations and as such we take our rightful place among the various liberation struggles.

But unlike these others, we are sacrificing a certain amount of our own movement's autonomy. You would be hard pressed to find an indigenous liberation struggle that would divert their own primary objective to save Animals in vivisection. But Animal Liberation and especially the 'militant' schools of thought therein have become sidetracked with cabooseing to other causes. Unfortunately even welfarists are better at protecting the autonomy of the Animal agenda, if only as an issue.

Our true strength in solidarity comes from sharing tactics and, when we can, resources (in a reciprocal fashion) with other liberation struggles -- not in compromising our own. And unfortunately Vegan Edge has fallen prey to this loss of primary focus.

I remember going to a show about 5 years ago... I think it was 'Shai Halud' and I was talking to this kid about coming out to the sanctuary to help the Animals and he smiled at me and said, "Walter, you're so message based," and then walked away. As I began delving into the lyrics of most so-called XVX bands post 2000, I see a steady trend where it's cool to get Vegan and Animal Lib themed tattoos, it's cool to announce in the coversheet that such and such a band supports a Vegan Straightedge lifestyle, and then it's really cool to never mention any Animal Lib or reasons for Straightedge in your lyrics.

This apathy would be tolerable to me if it was only affecting a music scene. But it's not. It diverts the message that replenishes the underground resistance. As a musician you can have great influence (Earth Crisis ring any bells?) And you also have a level of free speech that cannot be exercised anywhere else. You can sing in a song about shooting vivisectors in the face or even how to make a car bomb, but I can't write about those in an article. This is why tactically music to go along with the revolution has always been important in every time and place.

I would like to see Straightedge getting back to the business of being Straightedge. I would like to see crews and Vegan Hardline chapters become vocal about why drugs are exploitative and wrong and fight against them. And no, I'm not talking about getting ten of your friends together to go beat the shit out of a smoker. But direct actions on a local level against dealers and those that profit off of the ruination of humanity by the slowly poisoned death of intoxication. From the street dealer to liquor store all the way up to the medical industrial drug complex, drugs and drink lower inhibitions often leading to senseless and dangerous behavior.

Addiction is a nightmare not only for the user but everyone that loves, cares or relies on them. Most often serious addiction has no cure and very slim chances of lifetime abstinence. And huge drug companies like AstraZeneca are enormous contributors and funders of Animal experimentation. Many vivisector lunatics like David 'Tiller' Jentsch make a living addicting primates to street drugs when there is already a world of addicted human primates to observe and monitor. Whole countries like current day Mexico are engaged in civil war and bloodshed in the streets over drug cartels -- true narco-terrorism. But this is just the tip of the iceberg.

I would like to see Straightedge employ the same leaderless resistance and underground/above ground tactics as the radical Animal and environmental groups have for decades. And I would also like to see Vegan Straightedge mature and become multi-generational. The scene for the kids is great. But there is no reason to view Straightedge as only for the kids. Many adults that have been through the hell of addiction and survived or been the victims of loved ones' addictions or alcoholism definitely have a more real world awareness of how deep the rabbit hole actually goes. Therefore Straightedge should be viewed as a way of life which is good for all just like Veganism.

Which brings me to my next point. I feel that Straightedge should be synonymous with Veganism, social justice and respect for all innocent life. The immediate point of living drug free is to make the individual optimal, thereby bettering the world we come in contact with, because no person is an island. We affect our surroundings, many times more that we know. But for the sake of clarity and consistency, Veganism and Straightedge must truly be seen as extensions of one another. Meat, dairy and eggs are loaded with drugs in the form of steroids, antibiotics, hormones and more. Also when we speak about making the world a better place, it's only logical to extend that desire to the actual world, to nature and our Animal relations. Especially when we realize that our actions are interconnected to our surroundings.

Nor is Veganism a caboose on Straightedge. Since the mid-80s, bands like 'Youth of Today' and 'Gorilla Biscuits' were including the issues of vegetarianism for ethical reasons in songs such as "Cats and Dogs." And lastly on a tactical level we have seen time and time again that revolutionaries and revolutionary struggles must be clean and sober as a pre-requisite to success. Malcolm X and the Black Panthers are two contemporary American examples that come to mind. Even in the Animal Liberation Front Primer written in the 80s it states that no one active in the A.L.F. should use drugs or work with others that do. It briefly explains the connection between drug and Animal testing and ends the paragraph with, "Saving the Animals is what's important, not getting high or drunk."

Many people do not know what the best course of action is, not only in activism but in their day to day lives. Before you can effectively make a change in the world we must make changes within ourselves. Before there can be a revolution for Animals or the Earth, there must be revolutionaries, not a bunch of hipsters drinking micro-brews and Waiting for the Rev! Before the general population will adopt a disciplined caring and conscious way of life, we must.

There are incredible wrongs happening on this planet. By governments, corporations and individuals, and it's not a joke - it's fucking serious and demands our attention and energy! And these wrongs also demand that we make ourselves the best we can be. It means we know who we are, what we believe and what we are willing to do and sacrifice to attain those goals. It means we answer to the Animals first, each other second, other like-minded movements third and to our enemies and oppressors, never! It means we get organized and ferocious and support each other's projects and actions.

As Animal Liberationists we need to be either confronting Animal abusers directly or helping and caring for animals with our own two hands. As Straightedgers, we need to set a positive example of sobriety and help those whom we can, away from the quagmire and filth of addiction. And we also need to confront and fight against individuals and corporations that profit from this degradation. And as Vegan Hardliners we need to not only fight for Earth, Animal and human liberation, but for all innocent life with all the strength, courage, intelligence, love and intensity that we can summon. Because when we fight for an innocent's life as if it were our own, at that moment we are not only right, we are also above the law.

Vegan Straightedge rebirth, whatever it may take!

Interviews

Interview by Earth First! France, July 28th, 2009

Earth Crisis song "To ashes" deal with a topic which is quite hard, and it concerns you. Can you tell us about it?

Sure, the song "to ashes" is about an arson charge that I received in November of 1997 for burning down the home of a meth dealer and the meth lab that was in that house. This drug dealer had been selling his poison in my home town for about 20 years. He had half of the local police bought off and half of my graduating class addicted to his poison, including my brother, who had at that time been diagnosed with "drug induced schizoid disorder", which is just a fancy way to say he had lost his mind from drug abuse. I tried everything I could think of even talking with Steve (the drug dealer). but to no avail. So I decided to take the law into my own hands and I burnt his house to the ground in a fire that took 17 hours to put out. He was under investigation by the the FBI. which I of course at the time did not know. A couple interesting things happened at this point. First since the house was no longer a standing structure the feds were able to search through what was left of the place without a warrant. They found nearly 1 million dollars in drugs. Secondly Steve told on all of his drug dealing friends. So by the time it was all over I think it was 13 meth dealers in four U.S states that got life in prison. I myself did 4 years for burning down his drug den. I don't regret it one bit. My four years imprisonment was a small price to pay for such a positive result.

How did you become straight edge, and what does it mean for you?

I am now 33 years old, I have been Straight Edge for 18 years and Vegan for 13 years. I went Straight Edge mainly to rebel against my family. My father was a terrible alcoholic and my mother and brother were both heavy into drugs. I did not want to end up like that. I was like 15 years old and I heard a band called "gorilla biscuits" screaming the Straight Edge message. I loved it the moment I heard it! I knew almost immediately that this was for me. It was also through Straightedge that I learned about veganism Which I feel is the most important and worthwhile cause on this earth. As far as what Straight edge means to me? it means no drugs, no alcohol, no promiscuity for as long as I live. It furthermore means standing against drug culture and apathy.

Do you think that Earth Crisis' song reflects the complexity of what happened and of how you felt?

I think It captured everything very well, of course there is only so much message you can squeeze into a couple minutes of video. But Karl and the boys did a great job! Its really amazing to me to see my story in a song and video by my favorite band! I am humbled by it all.I am just happy if my story educates or inspires anyone.

Negotiation Is Over Interview, March 2011

NIO Interviews the Lone Wolf:
Go Vegan and Break Something!

NIO is honored that Walter Bond recently joined our collective as the Senior Editor of Militant Direct Action. His dedication to the enslaved animals and to this movement is unparalleled. Because of his courageous and effective assaults on the enemy, everyone knows the "Lone Wolf" as the state's latest prisoner of war. Now we want to introduce you to the person that we've come to know and love. Like many of us, he is unequivocal when he speaks. His beliefs and actions are consistent. And we proudly share a fanaticism in the war for animal liberation. But Walter has surpassed many in conquering his own fears and liberating his own mind — the transformation to warrior is complete. He may be locked away behind bars, but they can never imprison his spirit...

Lone Wolf permanently ended the reign of terror at this sheepskin factory.

NIO:

In many indigenous cultures, face tattoos are a rite of passage when boys enter manhood. When did you get your tattoo and what is its significance for you?

WB :

I got my face tattoo about two years ago and it has a lot of personal significance and many layers of meaning. So, let's see... where should I begin?

Well, much like most indigenous cultures, my face tattoo represents a very real rite of passage in my life — that passage was into warriorhood! It marked the exact moment when I put fear away like so many other childish pursuits. That's not to say that I don't feel fear. But I can honestly say that since the face tat, I have not made one fear-based decision, so that's liberating.

At the time in my life that I began really becoming enamored with the idea of the face tat, I was frequenting the tattoo shop quite often — about once every two or three weeks. Like many thirty-somethings, I had a decent job and a modest flat in the Capitol Hill area of Denver. But, unlike many, I was suffering from a profound restlessness. Almost every single day, I would wake up and be disappointed that I had not joined the underground for the total liberation of our animal sisters and brothers. The only thing worse than not knowing your purpose in this life is to know that purpose but not be able to summon the courage to walk the walk. So I was unhappy.

Everyday at my regular-guy job at Natural Grocers by Vitamin Cottage, I was more involved in my ALF daydream than my work. The epiphany that finally hit me was that, as long as I had this status-quo life, I would not follow my path. So my face tattoo also marked an acute change in lifestyle. Within a few weeks of getting it, I quit my job. I got sick of paying rent so I stopped that too. If I was out at night and a window offended me, that window received a rock! I very quickly began to understand that life is meant to be lived. Life is meant to be free. It's not something you plan to live in the future.

But, on an aesthetic level, my face tat is simply abstract. I have plenty of other tats that have particular meaning. So I just wanted my face to be tattooed, not a billboard — that's what my "vegan" throat tattoo is for.-WB

NIO:

Can you describe your transformation into a warrior? When did the "Lone Wolf" emerge? Was he always there?

WB :

My transformation into a "warrior" was, as I said, abrupt. But it's important for me to explain, however, that it was a very personal experience — not some empty platitude like "I'm a peaceful warrior." And it was a life-changing event. It was also a change that comes with very intense realizations. One of those is that I fully expect to one day die fighting, which I'm okay with. I don't think it's natural to die of natural causes. And, at this point, the worst thing I can imagine would be that soul-dead passionless "normal life"... not persecution by piece-of-shit cops or fear of death. I've become disgusted with certain aspects of western civilization to the point where going with the flow is more bothersome than resisting.

As far as the emergence of the moniker "Lone Wolf," contrary to popular belief, I never went by that or any other nickname. I came up with that name when I first started claiming my actions... on the spot with that first communique. Nor did I do it out of any need for notoriety. Compared to most, my communiques were very short and to the point. I used the name "Lone Wolf" to convey the message "hey, look what one person can do!" I was trying to forward a principle of action and empower others.

Everyone seems to sit around and wait for some mythical caring person to step in and right all the perceived wrongs they see all around them or they don't act until directed. I have found that when I rely on myself, I get way more accomplished than waiting to be validated by someone or some group. I can also say that the Lone Wolf title personally means that I am a free agent within animal rights. I ally myself with like-minded radicals, but I have been around and done enough tactically for animal liberation that I have no real mentors which, again, is very liberating.

That being said, just like my facial tattoo, there are other layers to that name. More so now than ever, I am convinced that the do-it-yourself attitude is the best. -WB

NIO:

I believe that fear is one of the greatest weapons the oppressors use to manipulate and marginalize activists. Activists allow themselves to be controlled through fear and many become puppets. You once said that your fear lies in not following your conscience, not in consequences. Can you explain this?

WB :

About a year and a half ago, my fear of any authority was trumped by my outrage at the casual murder that billions of animals suffer at the hands of speciesist human oppressors. It became trumped by my disgust at how humanity has become a plaugue of locusts upon Mother Earth and it became trumped by the disgust I feel at Euro-centric western civilization.

At some point in time, if you truly care about animals or earth or anarchism, feminism, queer rights, indigenous peoples or anything, fear must take a place on the back burner because it's the biggest prison of the mind that there is.

Ultimately, that's why governments need to lock up people like Maxim Vetkin, Braulio Arturo Duran, Adrian Magdaleno Gonzalez or myself — because we are not afraid! We lash out at the systems of abuse and, if we are not imprisoned and vilified or ignored by the media, then there is a very possible threat that others will become empowered. If everyone is empowered and truly taught to handle problems directly, then not only is it probable that they will not need the government, but it's certain that they will turn on it and destroy it. There really is no alternative.

Your apathy and fear either outweigh your caring and compassion or vice versa. In my case, it was not a decision to champion one over the other. I simply became fed up enough to start striking back and it's my solemn opinion that everyone should go vegan and break something!

NIO:

There is a great deal of emphasis in our community on ideology, political correctness, and ethical veganism. There is little to no focus on effectiveness. Since we both agree that this is problematic, do you have any ideas about how activists can empower themselves and move forward?

WB :

The big road block to effectiveness is that everyone wants to be able to be viewed as a good person. This is understandable because many vegans do care, at least enough to change their consumer habits. But, ultimately, effectiveness is what wins the end goal.

Look at it this way: if a bully seeks to violate you and physically harm you, being a morally-consistent and progressive individual will not stop you from getting your teeth kicked in. But being able to wage a vicious full-frontal attak ensures your safety. The end goal in such an encounter is protecting your security and safety as an innocent person and your right to be left alone by violent assholes. It's no different when you fight on behalf of another's rights.

What's truly moral is saving an animal in a cage from death. If you have to lie, cheat or steal to do that, so be it! If you have to break property or scare those directly responsible, so what?! I wish it could be otherwise, but it cannot. Go ahead, talk with someone that makes money off of killing animals. They don't care! But you will find that when you start harming their pocket book, you have their strict attention.

In answer to your question, we AR activists need to start with ourselves and begin getting in the habit of judging others, groups, and individuals by their effectiveness and actions instead of their words and booksmarts. We need to form this habit amongst ourselves and then demand it of others until we arrive at a day where someone says "well, I think this, that and the other," and everyone else's first reaction is "yeah, great... so what are you doing?" instead of "well, I disagree. I'm offended!"

I disagree with 321 farm animals dying every second. I'm offended by hundreds of things. And that means nothing unless it motivates me to act!

NIO:

Many are offended by our use of words like "war,"

152

"slavery," and "holocaust" to describe the conditions in which the animals live and those that our movement must engage. Is this terminology appropriate? Is it fair to refer to you as a "prisoner of war"?

WB :

I prefer real talk to verbose vocabulary for more than one reason.

First off, animal and earth death are not a philosophy. They are actual and evil.

Next, I don't want people to think that Animal Lib is an exclusive group of intellectuals. I want to attract warriors, not writers and thinkers. There is no war without the warrior. There is only a holocaust and understanding observers.

I prefer to be called a "prisoner of war" instead of "political prisoner" because I freely admit what I did. I'm not in prison because of politics — some are. I am not one of them. I'm incarcerated because I am an animal rights arsonist. I'm imprisoned for fighting against the everyday holocaust with fire and my true regret is that I got caught. But like a true soldier in a battle, I don't bring down morale by recanting or reversing myself. This is what I signed up for when I became an ALF operative.

I wasn't repentant when I was out there kicking ass for animals and, now that I'm in prison, my resolve has never been stronger.

Animal Liberation, Whatever It May Take!

NAALPO Interview with ALF POW Walter Bond

This interview with Walter Bond was conducted when Bond was first imprisoned for the "ALF Lone Wolf" arsons. Press Officer Nicoal Sheen carried out the interview almost a year ago to dive into the mind of this inspiring A.L.F. prisoner of war.

Nicoal Sheen:
Now that you openly admit to being the "ALF Lone Wolf," can you describe what it was like preparing and organizing alone?

Walter Bond:
Preparing for an action, on the technical end of things, was very easy. We tend to think of covert or illegal activity in the Animal Liberation movement as complicated. I personally found that to not be the case. Most of the supplies I used in the commission of the arson at the Sheepskin Factory I found in alleys and trash cans. All too often during A.L.F/E.L.F actions, incendiary devices haven't gone off. I learned from that and did not create a device to do the work for me. This also, I feel, further minimized any possible harm to life. I have never been comfortable with there being any window of time between leaving a target and a fire breaking out. It's important to know that it's "all clear" at the moment of incineration. There's too many unimaginable scenarios that can occur even within a 5 minute time frame. Mentally, it can be very difficult. The truth is, A.L.F. activity is illegal activity. When you're running around in the middle of the night destroying property, it takes nerves of steel. And control over your paranoia. I would become so hypersensitive to sounds during an action that it was bothersome. I dealt with this by wearing headphones beforehand so I was half deaf during the campaign. I could still hear but it kept me from stopping in the middle of my work to mind trip about a creaky building, or every little noise.

NS:

Were you ever skeptical about the successfulness of "lone" actions before carrying out one yourself?

WB:

I have never been skeptical about the effectiveness of working alone. Earlier in my career as a Direct Activist, I worked with others. I didn't like it. It always seemed that when three do what one can, the action becomes slow and sloppy and way too complicated. So that everyone feels like they did something significant. It's far more effective to handle business and get gone fast than to take extra time communicating with lookouts. Of course, for large scale liberations, that level of coordination is necessary. But not for economic sabotage.

NS:

Peter Young regrets not working alone when he was releasing mink before his capture and imprisonment in 2005, as he has stated in many interviews. Do you agree that working alone is "less complicated" and a greater advantage in an action?

WB:

Generally I agree. Of course as I said, it depends on what the objective is. The likelihood of carrying out a university lab raid single handedly is highly improbable. But often we underestimate ourselves and what we can do. After which we realize we didn't need the extra hand or snitch. But as they say, hindsight's 20/20.

NS:

In your essay "I am the ALF Lone Wolf," you state you chose the name "Lone Wolf" to convey "one person can accomplish a lot." Can you go into further detail of why you believe this to be important?

WB:

It's important to become self-empowered as Direct Activists. Because the leadership principle is a tool of the system. It plays directly into their hand. Contrary to what's portrayed the government is not as concerned with groups of subversives as they make out. The more organization, the more people involved, the easier it is to infiltrate or monitor. One person acting alone has to either get caught in the act or make a fatal error. Even in the legal Animal Rights movement, we are led to believe that you need validation by affiliation. Yet when I was in the above-ground, I turned more people to Veganism by talking to them personally. I have never turned anyone Vegan by giving an organization in another state a $50 donation. Doing things yourself is a surefire way to know what's getting done. If every individual Vegan and AR activist did that instead of waiting for a group to do it for them, animals would be saved by the millions instead of thousands.

NS:

What do you have to say to the critics of arson as a tactic in the Animal Liberation movement?

WB:

I would say they should be more concerned about the murder of animals and the Earth than the application of arson as a tactic. Furthermore, I would say I believe in Animal Liberation, Whatever it May Take! Not Animal Liberation, as long as people think it's OK! This is the A.L.F not Boy Scouts. Just because these critics will not employ arson as a solution doesn't mean it's wrong. I am not going to kill people to save animals but I would never speak out against it. Animals suffer and die the most cruel deaths in unimaginable numbers. My opinion is anything that saves them or stops others from exploiting or harming them is justifiable and anything that continues their Holocaust is wrong and must be fought. If you can watch footage of vivisection or a slaughterhouse and then tell me the solution is to write your congressperson or denounce us radicals that "risk our lives and freedom" to stop the carnage, then you are either a hobbyist or deluded about the level of evil you are up against. In either case these people should re-evaluate whose side they are on, animals or agribusiness. The two are mutually exclusive.

NS:

Why did you employ arson rather than another form of economic sabotage?

WB:

I used arson because the three most devastating elements to any standing structure are fire, smoke and water. With arson, all three do damage and it's hard to recover from. Even if you do not completely destroy a building, smoke and water (from putting the fire out) takes a long time to clean up. It's costly to the business. It also effectively sends the message that play time is over. I'm always happy when I hear about Direct Action but when it comes to property damage, breaking windows and spray painting an animal abuser's building is fun but doesn't send a message of Vegan Revolution.

NS:

Has there been or are there specific people in your life you would consider heroes? Why or why not?

WB:

Let's see. Malcolm X, Huey P. Newton, Leonard Peltier, Sean Muttaqi, Rod Coronado, Peter Tosh, and Zumbi. These are all my heroes because they fought what they believed, did not compromised and kicked some serious ass and were trailblazers of their time.

NS:

In your essay "I am the ALF Lone Wolf," you have criticized Vegans who are welfarist and stated that you "immediately felt out of place" at a local Denver Vegan meet-up. What are your thoughts and feelings concerning animal welfare? Do you find welfarism to be progressive or regressive in the Animal Liberation community?

WB:

I think a lot of people involved in the welfarist camp of A.R. mean well, but the approach is reactionary and regressive.

And good intentions do not stop evil. If someone is oppressing you or your family to death and you want to preach pacifism or employ luke warm tactics that's your own business. But this is Animal Liberation, as in other-than-human Animal Liberation and you have no right to plea bargain with animals' lives for political stature or organizational financial gain. I have no problem speaking out against welfarism because it often works hand in glove with animal exploitation industries such as awarding slaughterhouse designers cash money for "humane designs" and in many cases promoting animal use. I understand that there are a lot of upper middle class white people that feel guilty about their privilege and really want to seem like they are helping animals while being told repeatedly and daily that they are heroes of social justice, while also getting paid fat salaries. And never putting themselves or their reputations in harm's way. These god damned pretend friends of animals are more concerned with potlucks than productivity and property over life! And while the true proponents of liberation – the Abolitionist and Animal Liberation activists – educate people about Veganism (not Flexitarianism) and rescue actual animals' lives, some of us rot away in prison or live homeless and on the run from the Feds, these cowards (welfarists) are often our most vocal adversaries. In summation, I think welfarism is a detriment to Animal Liberation and I have no respect for it.

NS:

What are your thoughts and opinions about the label "terrorist" given to Animal and Earth Liberators by mainstream media, government and the oppressors? In your opinion, why do you believe society has accepted this label instead of challenging its validity?

WB:

When I was a kid everything was about the communists now the buzzword is terrorist. Like any Orwellian newspeak word "terrorist" has come to represent a whole spectrum of emotional fear instead of any rational definition. It's no surprise to me that A.L.F/E.L.F are considered terrorists. The U.S. government has been calling us that for two decades before 9-11. Because we are effective and can't be stopped, we get vilified. For instance, I'm facing 3 AETA charges, an enhancement of 30 years for being an AR arsonist. Had I been running around two burning things because of pyromania or some other sort of pathology, I would be facing considerably less time. The fact that the government invented such a ridiculous enhancement that can be used so broadly is testimony to their malice towards the bunny and tree huggers of America. However, at the end of the day, their personal malice of our movement and tactics is testimony to our effectiveness. I think that the general public accepts these labels of "terrorist" against anyone the government doesn't like because they are fat, lazy and increasingly uneducated – which is exactly how farmers send animals off to the slaughter.

NS:

What do you believe the Animal Rights/Liberation community is lacking, if at all, and how does the community overcome such obstacle(s) in order to save animals' lives?

WB:

Much of the A.R. community is lacking a sense of urgency and clear focus. I think the best ways to change that is to get back to basics. Start feeling this movement with our hearts instead of our heads. By our hearts I mean passion. When you see a terrible injustice, a profound evil like what goes on in any animal use industry. The proper response is not fear or sadness. The proper response to evil is outrage. Our focus should be on justice, Vegan justice.

NS:

Many people have said there is a failure to see and act upon the interconnectedness of our struggles, such as you mentioned in your essay "X To Whom it May Concern X." Reflecting on what it would be like to have a more cohesive liberation movement, what can we all do as communities to connect with one another?

WB:

Outside Earth and Animal Liberation, I am really not very concerned with connecting with everyone else's movement. Whether they use the word liberation in it or not. I have made that mistake in the past and it simply eats too much of my energy. I think that it's time that other "liberation movements" stop eating dead Animals and suckling the lactation of another species. I think that it's alright for us Abolitionist Animal Liberation activists to realize that we are the vanguards of social justice. Ours is the fight against the worst Holocaust ever! Billions and billions of the most innocent, the most defenseless dead! Murdered, tortured worse than any segment of humanity! As far as cohesiveness within Animal Liberationist circles, I would say enough with the politics. Left, Right, Libertine, Anarchist, lifestyles or religion, who gives a shit! Base your personal and organizational alliances on effectiveness for the Animals. On workability in action. Not philosophical denominations. If you are Vegan or going Vegan and are ready to kick ass for the Animals, you are my sister, I am your brother. Everything else is details.

NS:

Do you plan on writing a book with all essays you have collaborated so far?

WB:

NAALPO has my full permission to publish my essays as they see fit. I will keep writing them while dealing with my 3 arson charges and AETA charges. And after I am sentenced to prison, I plan on writing two books to help motivate, educate and agitate.

Animal Liberation, Whatever it May Take!

A Letter of Solidarity with the Informal Anarchist Federation

October 2011

Hello Comrades and a fraternal greeting to all those who fight evil, oppression and all government sanctioned authority.

To all those that don't chat but instead act, I am your brother. For far too long, theoretical, philosophical, heartless, gutless cowards have pretended to be the standard bearers of liberation. But liberation is not a book or a speaking engagement. Liberation is not a set of laws being passed and the system trying to include you in their corruption.

Liberation is the abolition of oppression. Liberation is a scream in the face of all those that seek to use you spitefully, for their own hedonistic ends. Liberation is a can of gasoline in your backpack and the power of Mother Earth in both fucking fists! When we die, there will be plenty of time for pacifism and silence. Right now it is time to fight. It is time to resist with all the power and force that love and hate can give us!

Those of us behind the walls and razorwire, those of us that have proudly fought, will proudly fight and never bow before any authority outside of our own have shown this world the path to true liberation with our actions. But armchair generals and keyboard commandos don't want actions, they want words. What a waste of time.

I have more respect for my enemies than the soothsayers, flatterers and hobbyists. Because at least my enemies are honest, at least my oppressors don't pretend to be otherwise and at least they know how to act and react for the benefit of everything their twisted black hearts hold dear. No scribe, scribbler, voicebox or bag of wind is a commander of anything outside of opinions and pieces of paper. That is why I speak for myself. That is why I strongly recommend that all political prisoners speak up whenever we can because when we stay silent, lesser women and men start speaking for us. Or worse yet, our silence makes us seem non-existent.

This government, that government, all government will always try to scare the many with the few. Because the truly free, those with a feral heart, can light fires in their cities even from behind their prison walls. And you know what? They can have my body, and that's all they can have. I exist, we exist, in the resolve of every comrade that is not scared and is going to employ direct action right now!

You can keep me locked away until this body is dead and decays and that's the end of their power! You cannot stop the spirit of resistance that animates me! You can't stop what you can't scare! Welcome to the insurgency!

Anarchism means "no more government" not "welcome to my bookstore"! Animal Liberation means opening the cages and then smashing them, not opening your mouth in like-minded company. Earth Liberation means a ski resort gets the torch, not another Rich Liberal building an eco-friendly house. And Human Liberation means ending the oppression of all civilization, not chanting slogans to news cameras.

In direct solidarity with the International Animal Liberation Front, the International Earth Liberation Front, the Animal Rights Militia, Militant Forces Against Huntingdon Life Sciences, the Conspiracy Cells of Fire. In solidarity with all political prisoners and to every warrior that has laid down their life or their freedom for true liberation. In solidarity with the Black Panther Party for Self-Defense and Move! Long live John Africa!

Animal Liberation, Whatever It May Take!

"If a man is truly free, he cannot be debased by the weight of his shackles."

- an unknown French anarchist's last words before being sentenced to death

Letter to the Animal Rights Prisoners Newsletter

August 2011

Dear ARPS,

Thank you so much for publishing my 'Why I'm Vegan' articles in the last newsletter! I've been meaning to write a letter specifically for ARPS but have been super busy (as busy as you can be in jail) with animal liberation activism. In Colorado I was sentenced to 5 years imprisonment for burning down The Sheepskin Factory after which time I was taken by airplane all around the country 'in transit' to Utah. I'm currently dealing with my last two arson charges and Animal Enterprise Terrorism Act charges. I've been as busy as ever writing articles about animal liberation, responding to supporter mail and doing interviews. It's uncertain what the future holds for me and how long my ultimate prison sentence will be. However that is all secondary to what is truly important. This earth and the animals suffer the worst abuses of human greed and injustice. As their self-proclaimed defenders, the well being of our animal relations is, or should be, our prime imperative. And I personally feel responsible to set a positive example of continued activism even if I can only carry on in the struggle with my pencil and paper. Still I have a voice, as do we all and a responsibility (as do we all) to use that voice for the greatest good. In the county jail I'm now in and will be in for the next few months I am not able to receive the ARPS Newsletter (but I'm sure I will be able to in the next facility). The last issue I read I remember feeling a sense of comraderie. Reading the letters and names and prison addresses of caring and compassionate activists from around the world always hits home that I am never alone. Recently I read the book, 'From Dusk 'Till Dawn' by Keith Mann. Reading those accounts of the early days and actions of the Animal Liberation Front was amazing! When I think about how many brave and life saving campaigns have been, and still are undertaken by the warriors of animal liberation, or the sacrifices of far better people than myself, such as Barry Horne, I am all at once awed and proud to play my small part in this movement. I am also reminded that it does not end. As long as there is an animal in a cage, we fight for their total freedom. As long as Mother Earth is seen as a commodity, as nothing more than raw material for human use, we fight! I don't know if I will ever see the day of animal Liberation that we fight for, but I hope someone does. As for me I'll keep struggling for that day in any way I can because it's worth it. Not for us, for others. Animal Liberation, whatever it may take!

Regards,
Walter Bond

Walter Bond's Address at a Fundraiser in Florida

On July 16, a fundraiser for Walter Bond was held in South Florida. Walter called in at 2 p.m. to deliver the following address:

Currently, NIO has been embarking on a campaign to end vivisection before it begins by letting students of animal research know that their future career path will simply not be tolerated by the true animal liberation activists of this world. People that make a living torturing animals under the guise of science are nothing more than sick freaks that must be stopped. It is my opinion that there should be an LD50 experiment done on the entire animal research community. Until that fortunate day arises, please support NIO as much as you can. Every dollar you donate will go directly towards the liberation of our animal relations and the abolition of their exploitation.

We must never forget the animal victims of human injustice. We must never forget our responsibility to defend their lives.

We abolitionists in this animal liberation struggle know that these are not complicated issues. We will never live in harmony with each other until we can live in harmony with the environment as well as other species.

Animals have the right to live free from human slavery, use, abuse and death. It's not rocket science. It's very simple. Still many factions, groups and organizations in the past and the present spend too much time politicking, people pleasing and paper pushing. Their logic is flawed.

Personal interest is the enemy of animal liberation. Our mandate is to defend their lives. The four legged and the furry. Those with wings and those with gills. Not to smile and talk and play on people's sympathies. If people's sympathy was so powerful than they would not engage in these horrors and slaveries to begin with.

But I must confess I did not write this brief address to give you a lesson in morality or to try and get you to see the logic of a truly revolutionary mentality. I'm reaching out to you to let you know that we exist. I want you to know that people like me exist. We know that every single abuse that our animal relatives endure at the hands of speciesist human oppressors is sick and wrong! We know that torturers and murderers don't stop because we ask them or even because we tell them. They stop because we make them! Unless you have saved an animal from death and watched them frolic with glee or run for freedom, then you don't know what's right or wrong. Unless you've walked the path of a liberator or warrior for these critters, then you don't yet know how impotent all other half measures are.

And I want you to walk that path. I want you to walk that path because it's necessary if we want to save animals, any animals from imminent death and subjugation. I want you to walk that path because it's long overdue and justified and I want you to walk that path because if you don't no one else will.

Once upon a time I was not so secure with my own abilities. I spent years talking to people, organizing and putting my energies into indirect activities, instead of animal liberation itself. I, just like all of us, bought into the glamor and hype of mainstream groups or key individuals having all the answers. While it's always wise to learn from the experience of others and employ tactics that have proven successful in past and current campaigns, the true tactical answers are in our hearts and in our feelings.

When I was younger, I used to build slaughterhouses for a living. One day while packing away my work crew tools, a hog got loose from the kill floor and made his way to our maintenance area. He was bleeding from the throat, scared and running for his life. I stood there and watched as he was beaten to death. While my fellow coworkers cheered and high-fived, I decided to shut my mouth. I decided to turn away. I made a deliberate decision to be polite, not risk my job or safety and just focus on "the big picture."

Now as I look back on my activism from this prison cell, my only lasting and true regrets are in what I failed to do. My shame is in my complicity. A couple years later I was a vegan, an abolitionist and an animal liberation direct activist. I vowed to never turn away again and don't you turn away either! The future starts in the present and every life saved is a victory. Ours is and always must be a selfless movement and it must become a ferociously active movement. If there is one pitfall that seems universal among the mainstream of animal rights, it's their capacity to think more than act.

Our resistance to the abuses must be physical. Think about that! In the very place you are at this moment, animals need your defense, protection and urgency. If you don't get along with other people or groups within the animal rights community in which you live, so what? Work with those you do or work alone. Don't ask the question, "what can we do?" - ask the question, "what must we do?" and then do not accept defeat. Then you will find that you have joined the most powerful and self-realized group of people on the planet. Those who span various social justice movements from various times and places. Those who come from every race, creed and generation. The true catalysts of change, the liberators!

Don't be so concerned with "the big picture" or "long-term goals of animal rights." The future is important but far too many individuals and groups assume the position at the steering wheel of this movement already. Instead concern yourself with the trenches, the hard work, confrontations and liberations you can win now in your own backyard. Remember, if you don't act no one will and what we do or fail to do right now is incredibly important. It's literally the difference between life and death.

Animal Liberation, Whatever it May Take!

Walter Bond's Address to the
Animal Liberation Forum 2011

"Animals need warriors for their defense not another
subjective school of thought. "

On Thursday, April 14, 2011 - opening night of the Animal
Liberation Forum 2011 at CSU Long Beach - Walter Bond's
recorded address was presented to an eager audience. The
following is his transcribed essay:

Welcome comrades to the 2011 Animal Liberation
Forum. I hope today finds you well and in good spirits. This
weekend you will no doubt network with many good people,
attend some great workshops and learn many tactics and
various aspects of the movement for the total liberation of
our animal sisters and brothers. As you participate in the
weekend's events I want you to keep a few things in mind.
First, security culture - had I more strictly adhered to those
principles and never spoke of an action after it was done I
would still be busy ruining animal exploiters' days and saving
actual animals from a life of pain, death for no reason. Instead
of spending time in a federal prison writing about what I
wish I was still doing. But you will hear plenty about security
culture this weekend. So you don't need a lecture from me as
well. I only mention it to caution you to take it seriously.
More importantly, I would ask you to reject "paranoia
culture". Paranoia, fear for no good reason, this does the cops
and feds' work more thoroughly than any breech of security.
Because without ever having to infiltrate any group of us,
clandestine or above-ground, there is cop working full time
in everyone of our minds. That paranoia dooms animals to
death by keeping us frozen in our tracks and inactive in the
most effective ways. The hour is late. This year more animals
will be slaughtered at the hands of humans for the most
trivial reasons than ever before in world history! And next

year that number will rise again. The Earth is suffering at the hands of Western Civilization! Crying out in pain at the avarice of technocratic wickedness! There is no way to save all this and our asses at the same time. We need to embrace and demand a spirit of self sacrifice, bravery and teamwork no matter what our level of involvement. When we review other liberation struggles be it the Black Panthers, American Indian Movement, Suffragettes, Zapatistas, or the rioters at Stonewall, we will see at once that self sacrifice, courage and ferocity are unavoidable if your concern is success. It is better to act on your own terms than to react to the security forces of animal exploitation. When we choose the battlefield, the advantage is ours. When we play their game, we cannot see the road ahead and inevitable wreck that is waiting for us.

I don't know about you but I got sick of playing games in the name of liberation awhile ago. Animals need warriors for their defense not another subjective school of thought. Which brings me to my next point. Philosophy. Over the course of this weekend you will no doubt meet and talk to various people. We don't all see eye to eye on many issues and that's fine. Please make animal liberation and a love of this planet which we all inhabit the glue that sticks us together. We vegans have a personal opinion about everything. Which is understandable because we are thinking people but perfect adherence to philosophical denominations is not needed to become incredibly effective. That's because things like loving and fighting are intuitive and can even become hindered by excessive definition. Whether you are at a rally, home demonstration, or part of an underground cell, the vegan fighting by your side in the trenches is your sister or brother until actions prove otherwise. My wish for every single one of you is that this movement lives in your heart and guides your every action because once it does no can take it from you. And no one can validate it for you either. Demand more of yourself than you do of anyone else. And don't just be yourself but let others be themselves, for that is the true nature of leaderless resistance. Let your activity be your voice, words are cheap and easy. The only reason my words have weight is because of the actions that back them.

When I have seen or heard of activists turning against each other or being divisive over politics, religion or philosophy I find it incredibly disheartening. Not because of confrontation, that is just a reality of life. But because at that point a movement dissolves into a school of thought. A rhetorical theorem. And while we contemplate the origins of patriarchy and matriarchy, a million animals get stabbed in the throat, broken by the yoke, beaten for not performing for a crowd, murdered in toxicity tests for Tide and Bleach, forced inhalation by Philip Morris and RJ Reynolds. While we debate about topics of human interest, the last of the forest falls and the water turns to excrement and the world bleeds to death! A movement must move! Not spend 98% of its time in stasis, planning and posturing and 2% of the time putting its back into its beliefs.

And lastly, a few words about levels of involvement! There are many ways you can help animals, but make no mistake direct action is the most powerful. By direct action I mean anything that helps animals, now. I once knew a young woman who would travel the countryside of Colorado and go to places of animal abuse like ranches, turkey and chicken farms and just act cute and repetitively ask for an animal over and over, persistently, pretty please with sugar on top. She ended up with so many critters she had to purchase 30 acres to house everyone comfortably. That simple and legal action had has more profound of an effect than a million vegans at potlucks competing with each other about who feels the animals' pain the most. Or a hundred activists that write me to tell me they wish they could do what I have done. Saving actual animals' lives, costing animal abusers money, stopping the exploitation by any means necessary, educating people about the total abstinence from animal products: this is where our most successful efforts lay. Direct activism, legal or illegal, is morally justified and it works. It saves life today instead of planting seeds or waiting for ripple effects in a hopeful future.

In closing, have fun this weekend, learn what is needful and let this be the moment where you resolve yourself to make a difference in this world and the lives of suffering, innocent animals that desperately need your actions and cannot even see your posturing. Remember its not what you think or feel, but your actions that make you either part of the solution or part of the problem.

Animal Liberation, whatever it may take!

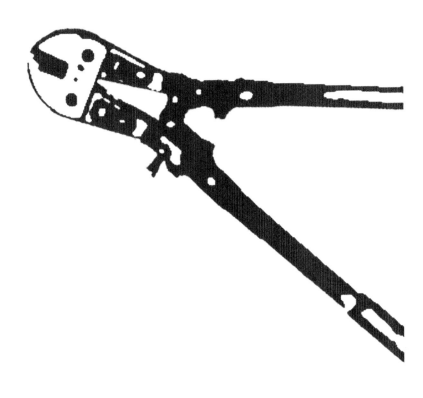

Special Thanks

It was over a year ago in 2010 that we learned Walter was not receiving support and had no support crew. Instead of being disheartened with the movement we offered our help and took action. Never did we think that rising to his aid would bring us this far into a journey of animal liberation. We can say that he has kept us very busy at times but in the effort he has also kept all of us inspired. It has been an honor to work with such an unapologetic individual for the cause and we challenge all of you to get to know him better.

Every time you write Walter you help create this community and make it stronger. As Keith Mann once said "If they haven't got prisoners, we have stopped fighting. If our prisoners are forgotten about, they have beaten us."

SupportWalter.org

~

A very special thanks to Walter and all of his bravery. It takes a dedicated person to take illegal action and a stronger person to speak out after being caught. Walter, we love you!

We would like to give a very special thanks to the following people and support:

Walter's Mom and Dad, Mickie Coyote and James Bond, for being the most supportive parents an activist could ever want in any lifetime.

Elizabeth Tobier for being the strength to keep Walter standing strong and his shield for protection.

Greg Kelly, Camille Marino, Nicoal Sheen and Dr. Jerry Vlasak for always making things possible.

Negotiation is Over and the North American Animal Liberation Press Office.

Also a very special thanks to Michele Mooney a complete support rockstar and all of Walter's Supporters. You are what keeps him going.

But like any journey as it unfolds, really this is only the beginning.

The rest is now up to you.

Walter Bond with his buddy Jeffery Thomas

CPSIA information can be obtained at www.ICGtesting.com
Printed in the USA
LVOW04s1127181214

419405LV00003B/141/P